T0290508

Career Paths in the Army Civilian Workforce

Identifying Common Patterns Based on Statistical Clustering

Shanthi Nataraj, Lawrence M. Hanser

Prepared for the United States Army

For more information on this publication, visit www.rand.org/t/RR2280

Library of Congress Cataloging-in-Publication Data is available for this publication.
ISBN: 978-0-8330-9989-1

Published by the RAND Corporation, Santa Monica, Calif.

© Copyright 2018 RAND Corporation

RAND® is a registered trademark.

Cover: *Civilians and Noncommissioned officers participate in the 2007 U.S. Army Research Laboratory Greening Course held at Aberdeen Proving Ground, Maryland. (U.S. Army photo by Jhi Scott)*

Support RAND
Make a tax-deductible charitable contribution at
www.rand.org/giving/contribute

www.rand.org

Preface

This report documents research and analysis conducted as part of a project entitled *Assessing Job Histories and Career Progression for Civilian Leader Development*, sponsored by the Assistant Secretary of the Army for Manpower and Reserve Affairs. The purpose of the project was to assess rates of career progression in different career fields in the Army civilian workforce and examine individual characteristics and job histories in the most commonly occurring Army civilian career paths, in order to better understand how career development plans may be tailored to different segments of the civilian workforce and used to encourage civilian leader development.

The Project Unique Identification Code (PUIC) for the project that produced this document is RAN167254.

This research was conducted within RAND Arroyo Center's Personnel, Training, and Health Program. RAND Arroyo Center, part of the RAND Corporation, is a federally funded research and development center (FFRDC) sponsored by the United States Army.

RAND operates under a "Federal-Wide Assurance" (FWA00003425) and complies with the *Code of Federal Regulations for the Protection of Human Subjects Under United States Law* (45 CFR 46), also known as "the Common Rule," as well as with the implementation guidance set forth in DoD Instruction 3216.02. As applicable, this compliance includes reviews and approvals by RAND's Institutional Review Board (the Human Subjects Protection Committee) and by the U.S. Army. The views of sources utilized in this study are solely their own and do not represent the official policy or position of DoD or the U.S. Government.

Contents

Figures

Tables

Summary

What does the career of a "typical" Army civilian look like? The conventional wisdom is that individuals who take civilian positions value the relatively high job security associated with government employment. Further, a common perception is that these individuals join the civilian workforce soon after earning a degree, spend a long career in the Army, and then leave upon becoming eligible for retirement. However, if many Army civilians follow a different career trajectory—that is, if they spend only a few years in the Army, or if they move among various Department of Defense (DoD) components—then workforce managers may need to tailor existing workforce management policies on hiring, training, and leadership development to account for these alternative career trajectories.

To investigate these issues, we identified the most common career patterns among individuals who entered the Army civilian workforce between fiscal year (FY) 1981 and FY 2000 and were on the General Schedule (GS) pay plan. We used a statistical clustering method that identifies patterns of career trajectories that are the most similar in terms of length of service, promotion frequency and timing, and transfers between the Army and other DoD components. After identifying these common career patterns, we examined the extent to which each pattern is related to individual and job characteristics.

Common Career Patterns

To identify common career patterns, we first defined key "events" of interest in an Army civilian career:

- Entry into the DoD civilian workforce
- Promotion milestones, defined as promotion from one grade group to the next: from GS 1–9 to GS 10–12, from GS 10–12 to GS 13–15, or from GS 13–15 to the Senior Executive Service (SES)
- Transfer from the Army civilian workforce to the civilian workforce of another DoD component

- Transfer from the civilian workforce of another DoD component to the Army civilian workforce
- Separation from the DoD civilian workforce.

We used an agglomerative hierarchical clustering technique to group similar trajectories together. To apply this technique, we started with end-of-FY snapshots from the Defense Manpower Data Center (DMDC) Civilian Master files. We began with records for all civilians who were ever observed in the Army civilian workforce between FY 1980 and FY 2015. To ensure that we could observe a sufficiently long career and identify an entry date, we limited the sample to those who were first observed in the DoD civilian workforce between FY 1981 and FY 2000. We also focused our analysis on those who were continuously in the GS or SES pay plans (or, between 2006 and 2010, on the National Security Personnel System [NSPS] pay plan). Since we aimed to trace individual career trajectories, we limited the sample to those individuals observed in the DoD civilian workforce for at least two fiscal years. However, as we discuss below, including individuals observed during only one fiscal year is unlikely to have changed the fundamental career patterns we identified. We followed the individuals in our sample from when they were first observed entering the DoD civilian workforce until the end of FY 2015, or until they exited the DoD civilian workforce.

Applying the clustering technique to this sample, we identified seven common career patterns among GS employees in the Army civilian workforce. Table S.1 lists the career patterns in order of prevalence (in other words, the pattern containing the highest number of individuals is listed first). Since the clustering algorithm groups

Table S.1
Common Career Patterns of Army Civilians

Career Pattern Number	Career Pattern Description	Percentage of Individuals	Percentage of Person-Years	Mean YOS	Median YOS
1	Short-Term	64.4	33.9	6.4	5
2	Mid-Grade	11.0	19.8	21.7	21
3	Low-Grade	9.5	19.9	25.2	25
4	High-Grade	4.1	8.2	24.1	25
5	Multiple Components, Low-Grade	3.9	7.5	23.0	23
6	Multiple Components, Higher Grades	3.8	7.8	24.9	25
7	Long Gap	3.3	3.1	11.3	11

NOTE: Percentage of Individuals indicates the share of employees in the sample who were identified with each particular career pattern. Percentage of Person-Years is the number of years of DoD civil service by individuals in the career pattern, as a share of the total number of years of DoD civil service by all individuals in the sample. Authors' calculations based on hierarchical clustering analysis using end-of-year snapshots from the DMDC Civilian Master Files from FY 1980 to FY 2015.

together individuals with either similar lengths of service or similar promotion histories, we used those similarities to create descriptive terms for each pattern.

As shown in Table S.1, there is substantial heterogeneity in the career patterns that Army civilians follow. Nearly 65 percent of the individual career histories in the sample are part of the largest career pattern, which we characterized as "Short-Term." Most individuals in this group are observed in the DoD civilian workforce for fewer than ten years, with a median total length of service of five years, and are typically in relatively low grades (GS 1–9). These individuals are largely observed in the Army, but some do spend time in other DoD components.

Among the cohorts we studied, approximately 20 percent of entrants were observed in the DoD civilian workforce only once. Had we included these individuals, it is likely that they would have been classified in the Short-Term career pattern. If the inclusion of these individuals did not change the career pattern assignments of the other individuals already in the sample, the share of individual career trajectories included in the Short-Term pattern would then have been even higher, at 72 percent, and the shares of each of the other career patterns would have been slightly lower. Even excluding these individuals, however, makes it clear that the majority of individuals who enter the Army civilian workforce remain for a relatively short time.

The next most common career pattern, which we characterized as "Mid-Grade," typically includes individuals who spend mid- to long-term careers in the DoD civilian workforce, with most of that time in the Army. The median number of years of service (YOS) observed in this career pattern is 21, and individuals are typically promoted to GS-10, GS-11, or GS-12 before leaving the civilian workforce. These individuals account for approximately 11 percent of all career trajectories. A similar share of career trajectories is found in the "Low-Grade" career pattern, characterized by a median length of 25 YOS, and generally without promotion beyond GS-9. A smaller share of career trajectories—approximately 4 percent—is represented by the "High-Grade" career pattern, which includes those with long-term careers in the Army civilian workforce, with a median length of 25 YOS. Individuals in this career pattern often begin in relatively low grades but are eventually promoted to GS-13 or above.

The last three career patterns largely include individuals who leave the Army civilian workforce for a substantial period of time—either to go to other parts of the DoD civilian workforce or to leave the DoD civilian workforce altogether—but then return. About 4 percent of career histories are part of the "Multiple Components, Low-Grade" career pattern. These individuals typically begin their civilian careers in the Army, in relatively low grades. After several YOS, they often move to another part of the DoD civilian workforce, remaining in a relatively low grade. Another 4 percent of career trajectories also exhibit transitions between different parts of the DoD civilian workforce. In this "Multiple Components, Higher Grades" career pattern, individuals begin in the Army and move to other DoD components, or begin in other DoD components and move to the Army, at various grade levels. Individuals in both of these career patterns spend a fairly long time in the DoD civilian workforce, with average YOS between 20 and 25 years. Finally, about 3 percent of career histories exhibit a gap from all DoD civil service, with a return typically 10 to 20 years later.

The career pattern names presented in Table S.1 are meant to provide guidance regarding typical career histories observed in the career pattern. They are not meant to indicate that *every* individual career trajectory found in the career pattern adheres to certain limits. For example, there are some individuals in the Low-Grade career pattern who remain in the Army civilian workforce for fewer than 20 years or are promoted beyond GS-9. In addition, the hierarchical clustering technique places each individual career trajectory into one of the career patterns. Even if an individual career trajectory does not match any of these descriptions exactly—for example, if the individual has a short gap in DoD civil service and is then promoted to GS-14—that individual would still be identified with one of these career patterns.

The fact that a large share of individuals fall into the Short-Term pattern is consistent with the overall length of time that individuals are observed in the DoD civilian workforce. Figure S.1 shows a Kaplan-Meier survival (continuation) curve, which tracks incoming cohorts of Army civilians over time and shows the probability of continuation (in other words, the probability that an employee will remain in the DoD civilian workforce) after every YOS. This curve is based on all individuals who entered

Figure S.1
Continuation Curve: GS Army Civilians

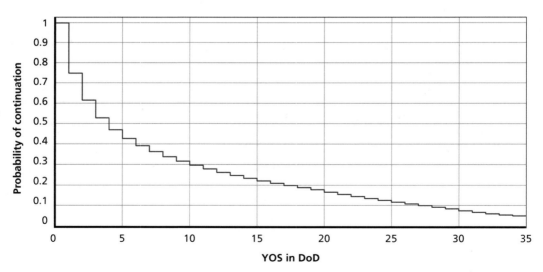

NOTE: Kaplan-Meier estimates of the probability of continuation among GS employees after each YOS. GS employees are those who are always observed on the GS, NSPS, or SES pay plans. Individuals are identified as departing the first time they are no longer observed in an end-of-FY snapshot. Entry cohorts from FY 1981 to FY 2000 are included, and individuals are observed until the end of FY 2015. Authors' calculations based on end-of-year snapshots from the DMDC Civilian Master Files from FY 1980 to FY 2015.
RAND RR2280A-S.1

the Army civilian workforce between FY 1981 and FY 2000, and who were continuously on the GS, SES, or NSPS pay plans. The continuation probabilities are based on the first time that an individual leaves the DoD civilian workforce. As this figure shows, the probability of continuation is less than 50 percent after five years.

Of course, since employees who remain for longer periods of time contribute more years of service to the Army and DoD civilian workforces, the share of person-years of service contributed by short-term employees is not as high as the share of entrants that they represent. As Table S.1 illustrates, the share of person-years of service represented by the Short-Term career pattern is only 34 percent, substantially below the share of individual careers represented by this pattern. Among all individuals who spent time in the Army civilian workforce on a GS, SES, or NSPS pay plan (not just those in the cluster sample), employees who spent five or fewer years in the DoD civilian workforce contributed only 11 percent of total person-years observed. Nonetheless, it is important for career program managers to understand that most incoming Army civilians are unlikely to spend long periods of time in the Army or in the DoD civilian workforce more generally.

Career Patterns and Individual and Job Characteristics

We also examined the relationship between membership in each career pattern and civilian employees' individual and job characteristics. We considered the following characteristics:

- Demographic characteristics: gender, race and ethnicity, education, and age upon entry into the DoD civilian workforce
- Prior active duty: whether the individual was a veteran or was retired from active duty military service
- Entry cohort: year first observed in the DoD civilian workforce (between 1981 and 1985, between 1986 and 1990, between 1991 and 1995, or between 1996 and 2000)
- Type of appointment: career (or career conditional) versus temporary or term appointment
- Career program at entry: based on occupation codes, using a mapping from occupation codes to Army career programs
- Number of years of federal service at entry (up to one year, one to five years, or five or more years)
- Whether the individual had supervisory status at entry
- Whether entry took place in the Washington, D.C., metropolitan area.

We examined the relationship between membership in a specific career pattern and each characteristic, holding all other characteristics constant. The results suggest a relationship between career patterns and a variety of these characteristics.

Women are more likely to be in career patterns that include short-term service, service in low grades, and a long gap in service. Black and Hispanic individuals are more likely to be in one of the low-grade career patterns and less likely to be in the higher-grade patterns, relative to white individuals. Asians are also more likely to be in the Low-Grade pattern or to spend time in other parts of DoD, at various grade levels. Asians and Hispanics are also less likely to be in the Short-Term pattern.

The youngest and oldest entrants into the DoD civilian workforce are more likely to be in the Short-Term pattern. However, young entrants are also more likely to be in career patterns characterized by eventual promotion to the highest grades. More educated individuals are more likely to be found in higher-grade patterns, which is consistent with higher educational requirements for positions at higher pay grades. Individuals with prior military service, particularly military retirees, are much less likely to be in the Short-Term pattern. They are also more likely to be mobile across DoD components and to exhibit a gap in service.

The characteristics of an individual's first position are also associated with career pattern. As we would expect, individuals initially hired with temporary or term appointments are substantially more likely to be in the Short-Term career pattern and less likely to be in any of the patterns associated with long-term service. There was some variation in career pattern across entry cohorts, with individuals in later cohorts more likely to be in the higher-grade career patterns. This finding may be driven by the increase in average GS grade levels in the DoD civilian workforce over time.

Some of the starkest differences across career patterns were observed by gender. To further explore these differences, we applied a method that decomposes the difference in the probability of membership in a career pattern into observable and unobservable factors. We found that observable characteristics, most notably occupation at entry and prior military service, could "explain" some of the differences between men and women. Women tend to be hired in occupations that are associated with shorter duration of service and lower grades. In addition, veterans are less likely to exhibit short-term service; since women are less likely than men to be veterans, prior military status may also account for some part of the observed gender differences. However, a substantial share of the differences between male and female career pattern groupings, particularly with respect to long gaps in service, remains unexplained by the factors that we can observe in the data. One key factor that we do not observe is family status, which may explain some of these differences.

Potential Implications for Managing the Army Civilian Workforce

All of the analyses in this report are descriptive—that is, we cannot identify the causal impact of individual characteristics on career pattern. Nonetheless, the findings above suggest a few steps that Army workforce managers may wish to take to better understand the drivers behind these findings, and that may help strengthen the leadership pipeline.

Collect systematic information about why employees leave the Army civilian workforce. Employees who leave the Army civilian workforce should be asked to complete a short exit survey. The survey could be offered to all who leave or targeted to those who leave during a specific time period. This survey should include, at a minimum, questions about the main reasons for leaving the Army civilian workforce. It would also be valuable to identify whether the employee has secured another job and, if so, some basic details about the new job, including location, whether the job is in the private or public sector, and the name of the federal agency (if public) or the industry (if private).

Understanding why employees leave can help Army workforce managers determine whether the high rate of departure during the first few years is a concern. On one hand, spending a relatively short amount of time with an employer is common in today's labor market; the Bureau of Labor Statistics (2016) reports that the average time spent with a current employer among wage and salary workers is 4.2 years. On the other hand, the exit survey may identify specific reasons for departure that Army workforce managers may wish to address. For example, if employees report leaving for private-sector jobs that offer higher pay or greater opportunities for advancement, or leaving for civilian positions in another part of the federal government due to lack of advancement opportunities in the same geographic location, workforce managers may be able to offer incentives to these employees to remain, especially in positions that are hard to fill.

Collect information on motivations for moving to the Army from another federal agency. An exit survey should provide information about why civilians leave the Army. However, understanding why civilians in other parts of DoD, or in the federal government as a whole, move *to* the Army can be equally valuable. The Army may provide better career advancement opportunities in certain occupations or locations; if this is the case, Army workforce managers may wish to build on these advantages in recruiting talent from elsewhere in the federal government, or to replicate similar conditions in other areas. A short entry survey, targeted at individuals who join the Army civilian workforce from another federal agency, could shed light on this issue.

Consider whether hiring outreach strategies could be modified to increase diversity in higher pay grades. While our analysis of gender differences across career patterns cannot be interpreted as causal, it does suggest that the higher likelihood that women spend a short time in service, or in lower grades, is linked with occupation, prior military service, temporary or term appointments, education, and other factors. If women are disproportionately hired into occupations that have few prospects for career progression, or that typically rely on temporary or term positions rather than career appointments, then it may be difficult to increase female participation in leadership positions. A focused effort to encourage the hiring of women in occupations that are associated with longer-term service in higher grades may improve diversity in the pipeline for leadership positions. Similar targeting with respect to prior military service or education credentials may also be effective.

Examine whether observed career patterns are similar across different segments of the civilian workforce. Our analysis showed that there is substantial variation in career trajectories across career programs; for example, individuals who enter the Information Technology Management program and the Analysis, Modeling, and Simulation program are more likely to spend longer periods of time in the Army. From the point of view of a career program manager, it can be valuable to understand the specific patterns associated with entrants into each program, in order to offer more effective career guidance to employees and to build a workforce with the desired mix of experience. Therefore, we recommend a career pattern analysis specific to certain critical segments of the Army civilian workforce, particularly those in which attrition and leader development are expected to be particularly challenging.

Explore whether resources are being effectively applied within the civilian workforce. The cluster analysis highlighted that there is a substantial amount of heterogeneity in civilian career patterns. Since the resources available for training civilians—in terms of both money and time—are limited, it is important that they be applied efficiently and effectively. A first step toward this goal would be to systematically document how training resources are distributed across geographic locations, commands, and career programs, as well as how they are distributed across individual career stages (for example, new entrants versus midcareer civilians). Further analysis could then examine whether the application of those training resources is associated with desired retention and promotion outcomes.

Acknowledgments

We are grateful to Ms. Gwen DeFilippi, who, at the time the research was conducted, was the Deputy Assistant Secretary of the Army (Civilian Personnel) and the Director of the Civilian Senior Leader Management Office, for sponsoring this study and providing valuable guidance for our analyses; to Ms. Paula Patrick, the current Deputy Assistant Secretary of the Army (Civilian Personnel) and Director of the Civilian Senior Leader Management Office, for her continued support; and to Mr. H. J. (Touggy) Orgeron, for his constructive feedback and his assistance in obtaining data. We are also indebted to Stephanie Kovalchik, who originally suggested and helped us to apply the statistical clustering technique we used. We thank our RAND colleague Matthew Cefalu for his expert advice on how to address some of the statistical challenges that arose in identifying civilian career patterns, as well as Martha Timmer, who provided programming support. We also thank Denis Agniel and Jennifer Lewis from RAND and Dan Ward from the MITRE Corporation for their valuable reviews. Any remaining errors are the responsibility of the authors.

Abbreviations

DMDC	Defense Manpower Data Center
DoD	Department of Defense
FY	fiscal year
GS	General Schedule
NSPS	National Security Personnel System
OM	optimal matching
OPM	Office of Personnel Management
SES	Senior Executive Service
YOS	years of service

CHAPTER ONE

Introduction

What does the career of a "typical" Army civilian look like? The conventional wisdom is that individuals who take civilian positions value the relatively high job security associated with government employment. Further, a common perception is that these individuals join the civilian workforce soon after earning a degree, spend a long career in the Army, and then leave upon becoming eligible for retirement. Consistent with these perceptions, the Army Civilian Training, Education & Development System (ACTEDS) is currently oriented toward employees who spend a relatively long time in the Army civilian workforce; Army Regulation 690-950 describes ACTEDS as a plan that "guides the organizational, occupational, and individual growth of Army Civilians through the full spectrum of the civilian human capital life cycle and entails a progressive series of TE&PD [training, education, and professional development] opportunities and assignments specific to a career program" (U.S. Department of the Army [2016], Career Program Management: Army Regulation 690-950).

However, if the behavior of many Army civilians does not fit this pattern—that is, if they spend only a few years in the Army, if they move among various Department of Defense (DoD) components, or if they spend long stretches of time in the Army without exhibiting substantial career progress—then workforce managers may need to tailor existing workforce management policies on hiring, training, and leadership development to account for these alternative career trajectories.

To date, there has been little quantitative evidence on what the career trajectories of Army civilians actually look like. In this report we take a step toward filling that gap by identifying the most common career patterns observed among individuals who entered the Army civilian workforce between fiscal year (FY) 1981 and FY 2000 on the General Schedule (GS) pay plan. To do so, we use a statistical clustering method that identifies patterns of career trajectories that are the most similar in terms of length of service, promotion frequency and timing, and transfers between the Army and other DoD components. We then identify job and employee characteristics that are associated with each career pattern.

Chapter Two describes the methods and data we used for our analyses. Chapter Three characterizes the most common civilian career paths that we identified, and Chapter Four examines the relationship between those career paths and employee and job characteristics. Chapter Five summarizes our findings and discusses potential implications for development of the Army civilian workforce.

Methods and Data

This chapter presents the methods that we used to identify common civilian career patterns and to characterize the relationship between an employee's membership in each pattern and his or her individual and job characteristics. We also provide an overview of the datasets used to conduct the analyses.

Methods

Identifying Common Career Patterns

We identified the most common career patterns among Army civilians by grouping together similar, although not necessarily identical, individual career trajectories. We use the term *career trajectory* to describe both the timing and the number of major events that occur over the course of a civilian's career.

The grouping of career trajectories into career patterns was performed using an agglomerative hierarchical clustering technique (cf. Ward, 1963), where the dissimilarity matrix to be clustered was created using optimal matching (OM; see Appendix A for details).[1] OM can be applied to data types that can be described in a sequence of "events" (Abbott and Tsay, 2000). For this report, we use the term *career trajectory* to define the sequence of events in an individual's career. OM defines the distance between one career trajectory and another as the minimum "cost" combination of insertions, deletions, and substitutions to make the content and order of the events in two trajectories equal. The "cost" of making each trajectory identical to every other trajectory is calculated for all pairs of career trajectories, and this matrix of "costs" is used as the dissimilarity matrix for clustering.

Agglomerative hierarchical clustering algorithms work in a relatively straightforward way. The basic principle is as follows. Consider the number of trajectories to

---

[1] We used the packages "TraMineR" (Ritschard, Bürgin, and Studer, 2013) and "pattern" (Maechler et al., 2015) available in the open source collection of statistical programs, R (R Core Team, 2015), to develop the Army civilian career patterns reported here.

be n so that the dissimilarity matrix is $n \times n$. In the context of Army civilian career patterns, the algorithm first identifies the two career trajectories that are most alike (that is, those that have the lowest dissimilarity). These trajectories are joined into a cluster of two, leaving a dissimilarity matrix that is size $n − 1 \times n −1$. The dissimilarity matrix is again searched for the lowest dissimilarity, which may result in either adding another career trajectory to the first cluster of two trajectories or putting two other career trajectories together to form another cluster of two trajectories. The clustering algorithm proceeds by forming clusters in this way until all career trajectories are agglomerated into a single cluster—that is, one single career pattern. A graphical depiction of the results at each stage of forming career patterns appears as an upside-down tree with unique career trajectories at the bottom formed into decreasing numbers of career patterns and ending in one single career pattern at the top.[2]

A fundamental question when conducting a cluster analysis is, how many clusters are there? This is essentially a question of granularity. In this context, the question is, how many different career patterns do Army civilians follow? One way to answer the question is simply to take the total list of career trajectories and form them into career patterns where every trajectory in a career pattern is identical to every other trajectory in a career pattern. As we note below, there are 64,075 such unique career trajectories in the data, so this would yield 64,075 different career patterns. This level of granularity is too detailed to aid in understanding Army civilian career patterns. Choosing the level of granularity (i.e., the number of clusters to represent the data) is essentially an art form, as there is no correct answer to be derived from statistics. We ultimately decided that a seven-pattern solution provided a level of granularity that captured key differences in career trajectories but was easy to interpret.

A challenge in conducting the cluster analysis was the large number of career trajectories observed. We identified 64,075 unique trajectories, representing 273,918 individual career histories. Calculating the dissimilarity matrix for more than approximately 45,000 trajectories proved computationally challenging. Therefore, we took a simple random sample of 180,000 individuals out of the original 273,918 individuals. Among the 180,000 individuals, there were 44,933 unique career trajectories. All results are reported based on this sample of individuals.

A second challenge is that there may be multiple observations (or groups of observations) with the same dissimilarity measure or "cost." In those cases, the exact career patterns that are formed may depend on the ordering of observations. To address this challenge, we randomly reordered the career trajectories 50 times and replicated the

---

[2]   The overall goal of Ward's method is to produce "the least impairment of the optimal value of the objective function" (Ward 1963, p. 238) at each iteration of forming a new cluster, or in our case, joining another career trajectory to an existing cluster. Ward's objective function "is the grand sum of the squared deviations about the means of all measured characteristics" (p. 238). The key to understanding the linking of trajectories to form a new cluster or into an existing cluster lies in the formula that is used to update the dissimilarity matrix. Ward's hierarchical clustering uses "an update formula based on dissimilarities to minimize the within-group sum of squares" (Murtagh and Legendre, 2014, p. 276). See Murtagh and Legendre (2014) for additional details.

cluster analysis for each reordering. We then examined the seven career patterns that resulted from the 50 runs. In 48 of the 50 runs, the same final set of career patterns at which we arrived (described in Chapter Three) was identified. There were minor differences in the exact number of trajectories in each cluster, but the overall distribution of trajectories across career patterns was similar. In the two remaining runs, six of the seven career patterns were the same as in the other runs, but one of the smallest career patterns found in the other 48 runs was not identified.

We also checked the consistency of career patterns identified for the same career trajectory. Over 50 percent of individual career trajectories were associated with the same career pattern in all 50 runs, and 95 percent of individual career trajectories were associated with the same career pattern in a majority of the runs. In presenting results, we therefore use the modal career pattern with which the trajectory was associated.[3]

In the present work, we used OM to determine dissimilarities in career trajectories and then used hierarchical clustering to find common patterns among trajectories. The "events" of interest in the career trajectories were

- entry into the DoD civilian workforce
- promotion milestones, defined as promotion from one grade group to the next: from GS 1–9 to GS 10–12, from GS 10–12 to GS 13–15, or from GS 13–15 to the Senior Executive Service (SES; or, in rare instances, to GS-16 or higher)
- transfer from the Army civilian workforce to the civilian workforce of another DoD component
- transfer from the civilian workforce of another DoD component to the Army civilian workforce
- separation from the DoD civilian workforce.

Examining the Relationship Between Career Patterns and Characteristics

We then examined the relationship between membership in each career pattern and a number of individual and job characteristics:

- Demographic characteristics: gender, race and ethnicity,[4] education, and age upon entry into the DoD civilian workforce

---

[3] We also tried summing up the probabilities that individual career trajectories were associated with each pattern. The share of trajectories associated with each career pattern was nearly identical.

[4] Race and ethnicity were missing in the end-of-year data from FY 2006 and FY 2007, and were coded differently before and after this period. In FY 2008 and after, there is a separate Hispanic declaration code; in FY 2005 and earlier, Hispanic designation was included in the list of races. To make this variable consistent over time, if an individual identified as Hispanic starting in FY 2008, we counted that individual as Hispanic, regardless of race. We also created a concordance between the two different sets of race codes to make them consistent. In addition, there were a few individuals in the data for whom race/ethnicity changed over time. We used the race/ethnicity with which an individual identified when he or she was first observed (or, if race/ethnicity was missing the first time the individual was observed, we used the first instance in which race/ethnicity was identified for that individual).

- Prior active duty: whether the individual was a veteran or was retired from active duty military service[5]
- Entry cohort: year first observed in the DoD civilian workforce (between 1981 and 1985, between 1986 and 1990, between 1991 and 1995, or between 1996 and 2000)
- Type of appointment: career (or career conditional) versus temporary or term appointment[6]
- Career program at entry: based on occupational codes, using the mapping from occupational codes to Army career programs as discussed below
- Number of years of federal service at entry (one year or less, one to five years, or five or more years)
- Whether the individual had supervisory status at entry
- Whether entry took place in the Washington, D.C., metropolitan area.

We then estimated a multinomial logistic regression model to examine the relationship between membership in each career pattern and each characteristic, holding all the other characteristics constant. We used the regression coefficients to estimate the average marginal effects of a change in each characteristic (e.g., gender) on the probability of being associated with each career pattern. For example, for gender, we estimated the predicted probability of being in each career pattern, conditional on being male, and the predicted probability of being in each career pattern, conditional on being female. The marginal effect of being female is the difference between the predicted probability, conditional on being female, and the predicted probability, conditional on being male. Standard errors were computed using the delta method.

As we show in Chapter Three, a number of these characteristics, including gender, prior military service, and career program at entry, are associated with a higher likelihood of membership in certain career patterns. Gender, in particular, is related to career pattern membership: women are more likely to be associated with career patterns characterized by short-term service, as well as long-term service at relatively low pay grades. To explore this relationship in greater detail, we applied a method that decomposes the difference in the probability of career pattern membership into observable and unobservable factors.

---

[5]   We identified veterans in the Defense Manpower Data Center (DMDC) data based on their appearance in the Active Duty Master File. However, since our records of the Active Duty Master File date back to only FY 1980, we are likely to miss identifying some veterans in our early civilian cohorts. To mitigate this challenge, we also identified veterans based on a combination of veterans' preference, veterans' status, annuitant status, and military service variables from the DMDC Civilian Master File. We identified retired military personnel based on either 20 years of active duty service (using the Active Duty Master File) or an indicator in the annuitant status variable (from the Civilian Master File).

[6]   We classified individuals based on their first observed appointment, but we found similar results when identifying individuals as having temporary or term appointments if they *ever* had a temp or term appointment.

The decomposition method was originally proposed by Oaxaca (1973) and Blinder (1973) to examine differences in earnings by gender and race. The basic idea is that observed differences in earnings can be decomposed into a part that is "explained" by observable characteristics, and a part that is unexplained. This method and its extensions have been used extensively in the literature to examine average wages as well as wage inequality. Recently, Asch, Miller, and Weinberger (2016) used the Oaxaca-Blinder method to decompose the differences between the probability of promotion to certain grades for male officers and the probability of promotion to certain grades for female officers.

In our case, we used the Oaxaca-Blinder method to decompose the probability of belonging to a particular career pattern into "explainable" and "unexplainable" components, for men and women. For example, women are more likely than men to be hired with temporary or term appointments; this is an observable factor that "explains" some part of the higher probability that women are associated with the career pattern we identify as "Short Term." However, there are also likely to be many factors that are unobservable to researchers—for example, propensity for government service—that are related to career pattern membership, and that may differ, on average, for men and women. These unobservable factors make up the "unexplained" component of the difference between the probabilities with which men and women are associated with each career pattern.

Here, we provide a brief summary of the decomposition method as we apply it. Our exposition broadly follows Asch, Miller, and Weinberger (2016). Fortin, Lemieux, and Firpo (2011) provide a detailed overview of the original method and its extensions, as well as a number of applications.

We can write the probability of being in a certain career pattern, Y, as a function of observed characteristics, X, and unobserved characteristics, ε, for men and women:

$$Y_m = X'_m \beta_m + \varepsilon_m$$

$$Y_f = X'_f \beta_f + \varepsilon_f$$

Note that the relationship between the observable characteristics and the probability of being in a career pattern depends on the group to which the individual belongs (in this case, gender); the coefficients governing this relationship are given by β_f for women and β_m for men.

Let β^* represent a set of coefficients based on a pooled regression of career pattern membership on observed characteristics, that is, combining both men and women into the same regression:

$$Y = X'\beta^* + \varepsilon$$

Then, assuming that the unobserved characteristics are uncorrelated with the observed characteristics, and that the expected value of the unobservable characteristics is zero, we can write the difference between the expected probability of career pattern membership for men and women as:

$$E(Y_m) - E(Y_f)$$
$$= \overline{Y}_m - \overline{Y}_f$$
$$= (\overline{X}_m - \overline{X}_f)\beta^* + \overline{X}_m(\beta_m - \beta^*) - \overline{X}_f(\beta_f - \beta^*)$$

The three terms can be interpreted as follows:

- $(\overline{X}_m - \overline{X}_f)\beta^*$, the part of the difference that is "explained" by the differences in observed characteristics of men (X_m) and women (X_f)
- $\overline{X}_m(\beta_m - \beta^*)$, the part of the difference that is not explained by the differences in observed characteristics, but rather holds the observed characteristics fixed at those observed for men X_m and reflects the differences between the coefficients for men β_m and the pooled coefficients β^*
- $\overline{X}_f(\beta_f - \beta^*)$, the part of the difference that is not explained by the differences in observed characteristics, but rather holds the observed characteristics fixed at those observed for women X_f and reflects the differences between the coefficients for women β_f and the pooled coefficients β^*.

We report the overall contribution of the "explained" term, and of the sum of the two "unexplained" terms, to the probability of assignment to each career pattern. We also provide a detailed decomposition of the contributions of the observed characteristics to the "explained" portion of the differences.

A key assumption in the decomposition is that the observed characteristics are uncorrelated with any unobserved characteristics. This assumption may be violated in our sample because of self-selection: men and women may differentially select into participating in the labor market or into joining and remaining in the Army civilian workforce, and this selection may be driven by characteristics that are unobservable in the data. In addition, one or more of the covariates may be endogenous, so the covariate is correlated with the error term. For example, someone with a higher propensity to stay in the Army civilian workforce for a long time (an unobserved characteristic that influences career pattern) may choose to enter a career program that offers opportunities for advancement (an observed characteristic included in the decomposition).

Thus, the estimated coefficients in the regressions may be biased.[7] One way to address this potential bias would be to use instrumental variables. However, in the case of self-selection, the instrument would need to affect the decision to participate in the

---

[7] Fortin, Lemieux, and Firpo (2011) point out that in the case of endogeneity, as long as the correlation between the covariate and the error term is the same for women and men, the overall decomposition will not be biased.

labor market and to join the Army civilian workforce, but not directly affect career pattern. Similarly, in the case of endogeneity, the instrument would need to be correlated with the covariate of concern, but not otherwise affect career pattern. Given the difficulty in finding such instruments, we note that the results should not be interpreted as causal.

National Security Personnel System

Pay grade is a key variable in all of our analyses. Between FY 2006 and FY 2010, many Army civilians were switched from the standard GS pay grade system to the National Security Personnel System (NSPS). Employees on the NSPS were placed in broad pay bands; in contrast to the GS system, which has 15 pay grades, the NSPS pay plans typically consisted of four pay bands (U.S. Army Civilian Personnel Online, 2013). GS promotion patterns are therefore not comparable with NSPS promotion patterns. Moreover, since the NSPS is no longer used, examining promotion patterns between NSPS grades does not provide useful information about promotion patterns for today's Army civilian workforce.

Thus, we identified "synthetic" GS grades for any employees who were on NSPS, using guidance on how employees in NSPS were transitioned to GS following the end of the NSPS program.[8] The basic process of assigning synthetic GS grades was as follows (Figure 2.1):

- If an individual was observed in the same GS pay grade before and after he or she was observed in NSPS, we assumed that his or her pay grade during the NSPS years was equal to the GS grade observed before and after NSPS.
- For an individual who was observed at different pay grades before and after participation in NSPS (or was not observed either before or after), we identified the list of "applicable" GS grades associated with each NSPS pay band, using the guidance on converting NSPS employees to GS. The "applicable" grades differed by occupation; for example, an individual who was in pay band 2 in the "professional" NSPS pay plan (YD) had applicable GS grades of GS-9 to GS-13, whereas an individual who was in pay band 2 in the "technical/support" NSPS pay plan (YE) had applicable GS grades of GS-7 to GS-10.
- To identify which of the applicable grades the individual should be assigned to, we checked whether his or her salary was higher than the Step 4 rate associated with the highest applicable GS grade in his or her NSPS pay band. If it was higher, we assumed that he or she was in that GS grade. If it was not higher, we compared his or her salary with the Step 4 rate of the next highest applicable GS grade in his or her NSPS pay band.

---

[8] Information on the conversion process was provided by the U.S. Army, Office of the Deputy Assistant Secretary of the Army for Civilian Personnel.

Figure 2.1
Process for Assigning Synthetic GS Grades to NSPS

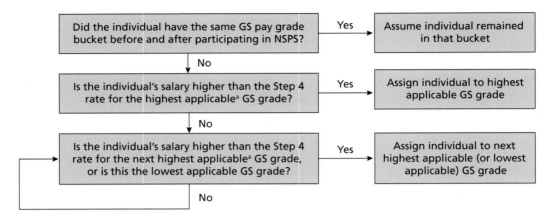

NOTE: Process used to assign "synthetic" GS grades to employees observed in NSPS.
ª"Applicable" GS grades are those encompassed by an NSPS band. We did not assign synthetic grades that were lower than the GS grade observed immediately before NSPS participation.
RAND *RR2280A-2.1*

- We continued this process until reaching the lowest applicable GS grade. If the individual had not yet been assigned to a GS grade, we assumed he or she was in the lowest applicable GS grade.
- In a few cases, this process resulted in the assignment of a synthetic GS grade that was lower than the GS grade in which the individual was observed immediately before participating in NSPS. In these cases, we replaced the synthetic GS grade with the GS grade in which the individual was observed immediately before participation in NSPS.

Data

We used annual end-of-FY snapshots from the DMDC Civilian Master File to construct career trajectories for civilians who were observed in the Army civilian workforce between FY 1980 and FY 2015. We started with an initial population of 1,261,858 individuals.

We focused our analysis on employees who were continuously in the GS or SES pay plans (or, between 2006 and 2010, in the NSPS pay plan). GS and SES employees have accounted for the majority of the Army civilian workforce during most of the past 25 years (Nataraj et al., 2014). Approximately 61 percent of the individuals in the original sample were continuously on a GS, SES, or NSPS pay plan. Since we aimed to trace individual career trajectories, we limited the sample to those individuals observed in the DoD civilian workforce for at least two fiscal years, leaving a sample of 640,684 individuals. However, as we discuss in Chapter Three, including individuals who were only observed once is unlikely to have changed the fundamental career patterns we identified.

We excluded entry cohorts prior to FY 1981 because our civilian data begin in FY 1980; thus, we were unable to construct a full career history for anyone who was already in the Army civilian workforce in that year. We limited our analysis to those who entered in FY 2000 or before so that we could observe up to 15 years of each individual's career, if he or she remained in the Army civilian workforce. These two exclusions resulted in a dataset with 277,534 individuals. We also dropped 3,616 individuals whose records contained missing or clearly incorrect key administrative variables, leaving 273,918 individuals.

Finally, as described above, we had to reduce the number of unique career trajectories to calculate the dissimilarity matrix for the cluster analysis. Thus, we took a random sample of 180,000 of these career histories.

We followed the 180,000 individuals in our sample from the time they entered the DoD civilian workforce until the end of FY 2015 (or until they exited the DoD civilian workforce). If an individual exited the DoD civilian workforce and then reentered during this period, we were able to identify the exit and reentry as long as the individual was absent during at least one end-of-year snapshot.[9]

In defining an entry cohort, we used the first year in which we observe an individual in the Army civilian workforce. However, since our data do not go further back than FY 1980, it is possible that some individuals served in the Army prior to 1980, left, and then returned. This concern is mitigated for later cohorts, as only individuals with a very long gap in DoD civil service will be inadvertently included in these entry cohorts. An alternative method would have been to include only those individuals whose files indicate no prior federal service in the year in which we first observe them; however, this would exclude those individuals with prior active duty service, or those who had previously spent time in other parts of the federal civilian workforce.

Mapping Occupations to Career Programs

The DMDC data include information on the four-digit Office of Personnel Management (OPM) occupational series code associated with the position each individual holds in each year. We used a mapping from these four-digit OPM codes to each of the Army's 31 career programs, as of March 2015, to identify the career program associated with each observation. Since a number of occupational series were matched to more than one career program, we first combined a few of the career programs into broader career program groups, and then matched each occupational series with a unique career program group. Details are provided in Appendix B.

---

[9] However, if an individual exited in, for example, October 2012 and reentered in August 2013, we would identify him or her in the FY 2012 and FY 2013 snapshots, and therefore not count him or her as having a gap in service.

CHAPTER THREE

Common Army Civilian Career Patterns

In this chapter, we begin by documenting some basic information about the length of civil service careers for Army civilians. We then present the most common career trajectories that were identified using the cluster analysis described in Chapter Two.

Length of Service

This section illustrates the length-of-service distribution in the Army civilian workforce using Kaplan-Meier survival (continuation) curves. These curves track incoming cohorts of civilians over time and show the probability of continuation among employees in each cohort after every year of service (YOS).

We focus on Army civilians who were first observed in the end-of-FY snapshots from the DMDC Civilian Master File between FY 1981 and FY 2000. We limit the analysis to individuals who entered in FY 2000 or before to ensure that we can observe each entry cohort for at least 15 years. We group entry cohorts into five-year bands (for example, those who entered between FY 1981 and FY 1985) and follow them until the end of FY 2015 or until they exit the DoD (or Army) civilian workforce.[1]

Our aim is to consider the number of years for which an individual serves in the Army (or DoD) civilian workforce. Therefore, we do not use the YOS variable from the Civilian Master File, as this may include service in other federal agencies, as well as active duty service. Instead, we define YOS as the number of consecutive end-of-FY snapshots in which we observe the individual from the time of entry.

The continuation curves show the time until an individual's *first* observed departure from the Army (or DoD) civilian workforce. For example, if we observed an individual in FY 1982, FY 1983, and FY 1985 and then counted the number of years between the first entry (FY 1982) and the first departure (FY 1983), this individual

---

[1] We used five-year intervals rather than considering each annual cohort individually, because we aimed to capture shifts that persisted for a substantial period of time, rather than focusing on differences that were specific to one particular year of entry.

would be counted as leaving after two YOS. About 14 percent of individuals exhibit such a gap in service.

Figure 3.1a shows the probability of continuation in the Army civilian workforce after a given number of YOS, by entry cohort.[2] Note that, since we observe individuals in the FY 1996–2000 cohort for at most 20 YOS, the continuation curve for these individuals terminates at 20 YOS; in contrast, the continuation curve for the FY 1981–1985 cohort terminates at 35 YOS. The careers of individuals who are still on board at the end of FY 2015 are *censored*, meaning that we do not observe how long they will actually stay in service. Therefore, the last few years of each continuation curve may be biased upward, as they are informed only by departure among those in the earliest entry years of the cohort. For example, in the FY 1981–1985 cohort, we observe those who entered in FY 1981 for 35 years, but those who entered in FY 1985 for only 30 years. Therefore, beyond 30 years, this curve does not reflect departures of those in the FY 1985 cohort.

Among the earliest cohort—those entering between FY 1981 and FY 1985—the estimated probability of continuation (until first observed departure) is approximately 75 percent after 1 YOS and 60 percent after 2 YOS. The probabilities fall to approximately 45 percent after 5 YOS, 30 percent after 10 YOS, and 15 percent after 20 YOS. If we include all years of service—even those that occur after a gap in service—the total number of YOS would be slightly higher than implied by this continuation curve. Although not shown in Figure 3.1a, approximately 55 percent of the individuals who entered in these cohorts were observed for at least 5 total years, while about 35 percent were observed for at least 10 years, and 20 percent were observed for at least 20 years.

Continuation probabilities for the FY 1996–2000 cohort are similar to those for the FY 1981–1985 cohort, at least for the first 10 YOS. In contrast, probabilities for the FY 1986–1990 and FY 1991–1995 cohorts are slightly lower than those for the earlier and later cohorts. The estimated probability of continuation for the FY 1986–1990 and FY 1991–1995 cohorts is approximately 35 percent after 5 YOS, 25 percent after 10 YOS, and 12 to 13 percent after 20 YOS. This difference is likely due, at least in part, to the downsizing of the civilian workforce that occurred during the 1990s.

Figure 3.1b shows similar continuation curves for time spent in the DoD civilian workforce (irrespective of component) until the first departure.[3] In this case, if an individual leaves the Army civilian workforce but immediately joins the civilian workforce of another DoD component, the individual is counted as continuing in the DoD civilian workforce. Thus, continuation probabilities are slightly higher at any given YOS, but the general pattern remains the same.

---

[2]   A log-rank test finds that the curves are statistically different across entry cohorts ($p < .0001$).

[3]   As with the survival curves for Army civilian service only, a log-rank test finds that the curves are statistically different across entry cohorts ($p < .0001$).

Figure 3.1a
Continuation Curves: Army Civilians by Entry Cohort

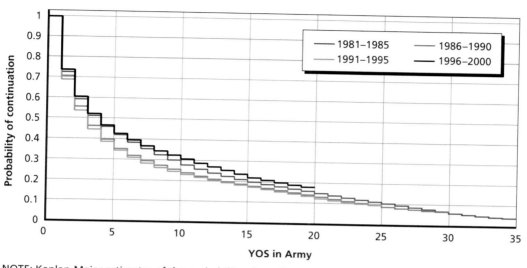

NOTE: Kaplan-Meier estimates of the probability of continuation in the Army civilian workforce after each YOS. Individuals are identified as departing the first time they are no longer observed in an end-of-FY snapshot. Each curve shows a different entry cohort, and individuals are observed until the end of FY 2015 or until they leave the Army civilian workforce. Authors' calculations based on end-of-year snapshots from the DMDC Civilian Master Files from FY 1980 to FY 2015.
RAND RR2280A-3.1a

Figure 3.1b
Continuation Curves: Army Civilians in DoD Civilian Workforce, by Entry Cohort

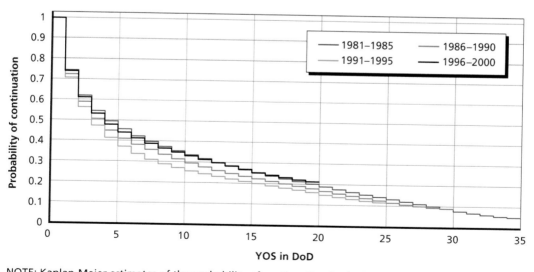

NOTE: Kaplan-Meier estimates of the probability of continuation in the DoD civilian workforce after each YOS. Individuals are identified as departing the first time they are no longer observed in an end-of-FY snapshot. Each curve shows a different entry cohort, and individuals are observed until the end of FY 2015 or until they leave the DoD civilian workforce. Authors' calculations based on end-of-year snapshots from the DMDC Civilian Master Files from FY 1980 to FY 2015.
RAND RR2280A-3.1b

In Figure 3.1c, we compare continuation curves for time spent in the DoD civilian workforce, among various subgroups. The blue line in Figure 3.1c shows the continuation curve for all employees; this is the same sample as shown in Figure 3.1b, but we combine all entry cohorts between FY 1981 and FY 2000. The red line shows the continuation curve for employees who were always observed in the GS, SES, or NSPS pay plans. These employees accounted for about 60 percent of individuals in the entry cohorts from FY 1981 to FY 2000. Continuation probabilities to 5, 10, and 20 YOS are similar for these individuals.

The red and blue curves include not only employees hired with career or career conditional appointments but also those hired on a temporary basis or with term appointments who would be likely to serve for relatively short periods of time. The yellow line shows continuation rates only for those employees hired with either career or career conditional appointments. Among these individuals, the probability of continuation after 5 YOS is about 55 percent (10 percentage points higher than the overall group). Similarly, after 10 YOS, the probability of continuation is close to 40 percent, compared with 30 percent for the overall group.

Figure 3.1c
Continuation Curves: Army Civilians in DoD Civilian Workforce, by Employee Group

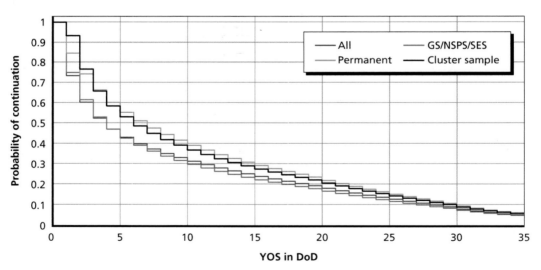

NOTE: Kaplan-Meier estimates of the probability of continuation in the DoD civilian workforce after each YOS. "All" indicates all employees who entered the Army civilian workforce between FY 1981 and FY 2000; "GS/NSPS/SES" indicates those who are always observed on the GS, NSPS, or SES pay plans; "Permanent" indicates those who were initially hired on a career or career conditional appointment; and "Cluster sample" indicates those included in the cluster analysis. Individuals are identified as departing the first time they are no longer observed in an end-of-FY snapshot, and are observed until the end of FY 2015 or until they leave the DoD civilian workforce. Authors' calculations based on end-of-year snapshots from the DMDC Civilian Master Files from FY 1980 to FY 2015.
RAND RR2280A-3.1c

Finally, the black line shows continuation probabilities for the 180,000 individuals in the sample used for the cluster analysis, as described in Chapter Two. We limited the sample to those observed for at least two years; however, since the continuation curve is based on the time to *first* observed departure, some of these individuals are identified as having left after only one year. The probabilities of continuation after 5 years, 10 years, and 20 years (approximately 55 percent, 40 percent, and 20 percent, respectively) are somewhat higher than the rates for the overall population of GS/SES/NSPS employees.

Compared to that overall population, a slightly smaller share (35 percent) in the cluster sample were initially hired on temporary or term appointments. This difference is likely due to the restriction that individuals in the sample be observed for at least two years. In fact, the 5-year, 10-year, and 20-year continuation probabilities for individuals in the sample are similar to those observed among the population of GS/SES/NSPS employees with career appointments.

Common Career Patterns

Using the hierarchical clustering technique described in Chapter Two, we find that Army civilians exhibit substantial heterogeneity in career patterns. Table 3.1 presents a summary of the seven career patterns we identified. The patterns are listed in order of prevalence (in other words, the pattern containing the highest number of individuals is listed first). The hierarchical clustering approach groups together individual career trajectories based on observed entry, exit, intercomponent transfers, and promotion events in each individual's career. It therefore tends to group together individuals with similar lengths of service or similar promotion histories. We used these similarities to create descriptive terms for each career pattern.

Nearly 65 percent of the individual career histories in the sample were part of the largest career pattern, which we characterize as "Short-Term." Most individuals in this group are observed in the DoD civilian workforce for fewer than ten years, with a median total length of service of five years, and are typically in relatively low grades (GS 1–9). These individuals are generally observed in the Army, but some do spend time in other DoD components.

Since our focus is on tracing individual career trajectories, we excluded individuals who were observed only once in the DoD civilian workforce. However, these individuals make up a sizable share—approximately 20 percent—of the FY 1981–2000 entry cohorts that were always observed on the GS, NSPS, or SES pay plans. If we assume that these individuals would have been included in the Short-Term career pattern, and that none of the individuals currently in the sample would have been assigned to different career patterns, then the share of individual career trajectories included in this pattern would have been 72 percent, and the shares of the career patterns described below would have been slightly smaller.[4] Regardless of whether we include or exclude these individuals, though, the majority of entrants into the Army civilian workforce leave within a relatively short time.

The next most common career pattern, which we characterize as "Mid-Grade," typically includes individuals who spend mid- to long-term careers in the DoD civilian workforce, with most of that time in the Army. The median number of YOS observed in this career pattern is 21, and individuals are typically promoted to GS-10, GS-11, or GS-12 before leaving the civilian workforce. These individuals account for approximately 11 percent of all career trajectories. A similar share of career trajectories is found in the "Low-Grade" career pattern, which is characterized by service of 20 years or more, with a median length of 25 YOS, and generally without promotion beyond GS-9. A smaller share of career trajectories—approximately 4 percent—is represented by the "High-Grade" career pattern, which includes those who typically spend long-term careers in the Army civilian workforce, with a median length of 25 YOS. Individuals in this career pattern often begin in relatively low grades but are eventually promoted to GS-13 or above.

The last three career patterns largely include individuals who leave the Army civilian workforce for a substantial period of time—either to go to other parts of the DoD civilian workforce or to leave the DoD civilian workforce altogether but then return. About 4 percent of career histories are part of the "Multiple Components, Low-Grade" career pattern. These individuals typically begin their civilian workforce careers in the Army, in relatively low grades. After several YOS, they often move to another part of the DoD civilian workforce, remaining in a relatively low grade. Another 4 percent of career trajectories also exhibit transitions between different parts of the DoD civilian workforce. In this "Multiple Components, Higher Grades" career pattern, individuals begin in the Army and move to other DoD components, or begin in other DoD services and move to the Army, at various grade levels. Individuals in both of these career patterns tend to spend a fairly long time in the DoD civilian workforce, with average YOS between 20 and 25 years. Finally, about 3 percent of career histories exhibit a gap from all DoD civil service, with a return 10 to 20 years later. Overall, the median number of YOS spent in the DoD civilian workforce, including time both before and after the gap, is 11.

Although the Short-Term career pattern accounts for about two-thirds of individual career trajectories, these individuals spend a relatively short time in service. Thus,

---

[4]   To calculate this share, we first multiplied each of the career pattern shares by 0.8, to account for the one-observation career trajectories that represent 20 percent of all individual trajectories. In the case of the Short-Term pattern, this resulted in a new share of 51.5 percent ($64.4 \times 0.8 = 51.5$). We then assumed that all of the one-observation trajectories would be in the Short-Term pattern, resulting in a total share of 71.5 percent ($51.5 + 20$). This estimate assumes that the inclusion of these individuals observed for one year would not have changed the career pattern assignments of the other individuals already in the sample. It is possible that some of those currently assigned to the Short-Term pattern would have moved to other career patterns, so our estimate may be regarded as an upper bound.

this career pattern accounts for only about one-third of the total number of person-years of DoD civil service observed among all individuals in our sample. Conversely, the Mid-Grade and Low-Grade career patterns each account for about 10 percent of individual careers but about 20 percent of person-years. Similarly, the High-Grade career pattern accounts for 4 percent of individual careers but 8 percent of person-years. Since individuals in the Multiple Components career patterns tend to have relatively long careers when the DoD as a whole is considered, each of these career patterns accounts for 7 to 8 percent of person-years. Finally, the Long Gap career pattern represents a similar share of person-years and individual careers (3 percent).

More generally, even within the Short-Term career pattern, those who spend ten or fewer years in service make up 80 percent of the total number of individuals but contribute only 58 percent of person-years, because they spend less time in the DoD civilian workforce. Those who spend five or fewer years in service account for 55 percent of individuals but only 27 percent of person-years. For the sample as a whole, those who spend ten or fewer years in service make up 55 percent of the total number of individuals but contribute only 21 percent of person-years, while those who spend five or fewer years make up 35 percent of individuals but account for only 9 percent of person-years.

The career pattern names presented in Table 3.1 are meant to provide guidance regarding typical career histories observed in the career pattern. They are not meant to indicate that every individual career trajectory found in the career pattern adheres to certain limits. For example, there are some individuals in the Low-Grade career pattern who remained in the Army civilian workforce for fewer than 20 years or were promoted beyond GS-9.

Table 3.1
Common Career Patterns of Army Civilians

Career Pattern Number	Career Pattern Description	Percentage of Individual Careers	Percentage of Person-Years	Mean YOS	Median YOS
1	Short-Term	64.4	33.9	6.4	5
2	Mid-Grade	11.0	19.8	21.7	21
3	Low-Grade	9.5	19.9	25.2	25
4	High-Grade	4.1	8.2	24.1	25
5	Multiple Components, Low-Grade	3.9	7.5	23.0	23
6	Multiple Components, Higher Grades	3.8	7.8	24.9	25
7	Long Gap	3.3	3.1	11.3	11

NOTE: Percentage of Individuals Careers indicates the share of employees in the sample who were identified with each particular career pattern. Percentage of Person-Years is the number of years of DoD civil service by individuals in the career pattern, as a share of the total number of years of DoD civil service by all individuals in the sample. Authors' calculations based on hierarchical clustering analysis using end-of-year snapshots from the DMDC Civilian Master Files from FY 1980 to FY 2015.

In addition, the hierarchical clustering technique places each individual career history into one of the career patterns. Even if an individual career history does not match any of these descriptions exactly—for example, if the individual has a short gap in DoD civil service and is then promoted to GS-14—that individual would still be identified with one of these career patterns.

To illustrate this point, Figure 3.2 shows the share of career trajectories in each career pattern, by total number of YOS observed in the DoD civilian workforce. As we would expect, two-thirds of those who are observed in the DoD civilian workforce for a short period of time are identified as being part of the Short-Term career pattern, but some are instead grouped with each of the other career patterns. Similarly, those with 12 to 15 YOS are typically found in the Mid-Grade and Low-Grade career patterns, but a few are found in the Short-Term or Long Gap career patterns. The reason for this variation is that our approach groups together careers based on examining a "dissimilarity score" for each pair of careers. That score is driven by entry and exit patterns, intercomponent transfers, and promotion patterns. Two career patterns may appear similar, for example, in terms of length of service but less similar in terms of promotion timing. At the same time, several different pairs of careers may have the same dissimilarity scores, so the grouping in that case may take different forms.

Figure 3.2
Distribution of Career Patterns by YOS

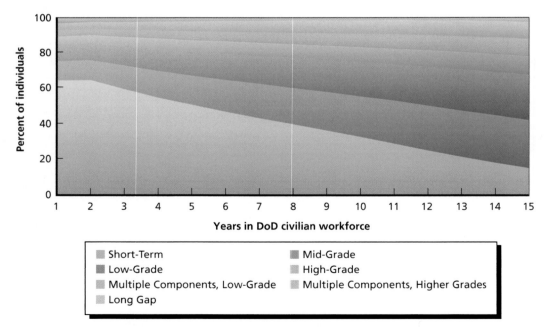

NOTE: Percentage of individuals with the number of years of DoD civil service shown on the horizontal axis who are identified with each career pattern. Authors' calculations based on hierarchical clustering analysis using end-of-year snapshots from the DMDC Civilian Master Files from FY 1980 to FY 2015.
RAND RR2280A-3.2

Below, we provide more detail on the nature of the career trajectories associated with each career pattern.

Career Pattern 1: Short-Term

We begin by showing the 50 most frequent career trajectories in the Short-Term career pattern. As discussed in Chapter Two, we conducted the clustering analysis 50 times and assigned individuals based on the modal career pattern to which they were assigned. Figure 3.3a shows results from one instance of the clustering, but results from other instances are similar.

Figure 3.3a
Fifty Most Common Career Trajectories: Short-Term

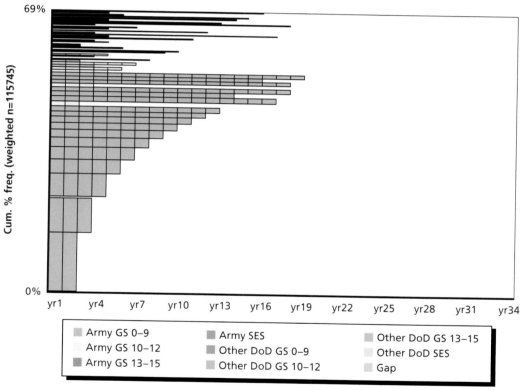

NOTE: Results from one replication of the hierarchical cluster analysis showing the 50 most common career trajectories of individuals identified with the Short-Term career pattern. The number of bars, from left to right, indicates the number of years since the individual was first observed, as shown on the horizontal axis. The height of the bar indicates how many individuals share the given trajectory. The "n" in the vertical axis label indicates the total number of individuals assigned to this career pattern in this replication. The percentage shown at the top of the vertical axis indicates the percentage of all unique career trajectories in the career pattern that are captured by the 50 most frequent career trajectories, which are shown in the figure. Authors' calculations based on hierarchical clustering analysis using end-of-year snapshots from the DMDC Civilian Master Files from FY 1980 to FY 2015.
RAND RR2280A-3.3a

In Figure 3.3a, each row represents a career history pattern, including length of service, time to each promotion event, separation, reentry, and transfers between the Army and other parts of the DoD civilian workforce. The number of bars, from left to right, indicates the number of years since the individual was first observed, as shown on the horizontal axis. Multiple individuals may share the same career history; the height of the bar indicates how many individuals share the given trajectory.

Consider the lowest sequence in Figure 3.3a. This sequence represents individuals who spent two YOS in the DoD.[5] The legend indicates that in both YOS, these individuals were observed in relatively low grades (GS 1–9) and were in the Army civilian workforce. This is the most common career trajectory in this career pattern, so the bar is fairly tall. The sequences are ordered from the most common (at the bottom) to the least common (at the top).

The "weighted n" in the vertical axis label indicates the total number of individuals assigned to this career pattern (in this instance, 115,745 out of 180,000).[6] The percentage shown at the top of the vertical axis is the percentage of all individuals in the career pattern captured by the 50 most frequent career trajectories. The higher this percentage, the less heterogeneous the careers of the individuals in the career pattern.

The 50 most common career trajectories represent 69 percent of the individuals in the Short-Term career pattern. Most of these individuals have careers of fewer than 10 years, although some do extend to 15 or more years. The distribution of length of service is illustrated more clearly in Figure 3.3b, which shows the continuation curve for all individuals in this career pattern. Similar to the previous continuation curves, Figure 3.3b is based on the observed time to an individual's first departure from the DoD civilian workforce. As noted above, although we limit the sample to include only those observed at least twice, a few of these individuals left after one year and then returned. The probability of continuation is 40 percent after five YOS and 15 percent after 10 YOS.

Over 90 percent of the individuals in this career pattern were initially seen in a relatively low grade (GS 1–9). Although it cannot easily be seen from the 50 most common patterns in Figure 3.3a, some individuals (about 20 percent) either started in or were promoted to higher grades (typically GS 10–12). A sizable share (18 percent) were also observed in the civilian workforce in other DoD components at some point, typically in GS 1–9. However, if we examine the total number of person-years associ-

---

5   Recall that we constrain our sample to individuals who are observed for a minimum of two years.

6   The term "weighted" refers to the fact that since some individuals have the same career trajectories, each trajectory is weighted by the number of individuals who have that trajectory. In Figure 3.3a, "weighted n=115745" indicates that 115,745 individuals were in this pattern, although the number of unique trajectories they exhibited was fewer than 115,745.

Figure 3.3b
Continuation Curve: Short-Term

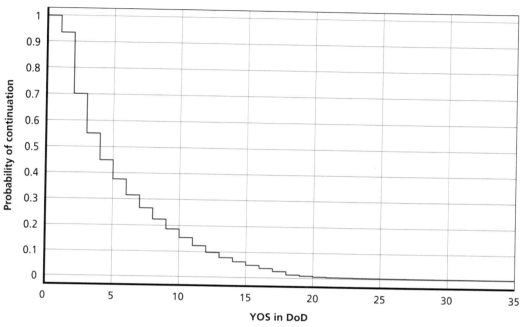

NOTE: Kaplan-Meier estimates of the continuation probabilities after each year of service for employees identified with the Short-Term career pattern in the hierarchical cluster analysis. Individuals are identified as departing the first time they are no longer observed in an end-of-FY snapshot, and are observed until the end of FY 2015 or until they leave the DoD civilian workforce. Authors' calculations based on end-of-year snapshots from the DMDC Civilian Master Files from FY 1980 to FY 2015.
RAND RR2280A-3.3b

ated with this career pattern, over 75 percent are associated with service in GS 1–9 in the Army.

Taken together, these points indicate that this career pattern is characterized by individuals who entered the Army civilian workforce at relatively low grades and stayed for relatively short periods of time, potentially spending some time in other DoD components. They then left the DoD civilian workforce altogether and were not observed to rejoin during the sample period.

Career Pattern 2: Mid-Grade

Figure 3.4a shows the 50 most frequent career trajectories in the Mid-Grade career pattern. Whereas in the Short-Term career pattern the top 50 trajectories represented 69 percent of all trajectories, the top 50 trajectories in the Mid-Grade career pattern represent only 15.6 percent of all trajectories. In other words, individual trajectories are much more heterogeneous in this career pattern.

As shown in Figures 3.4a and 3.4b, most individuals in this career pattern remained in the DoD civilian workforce for at least 10 years. The probability of continuation is 55 percent after 20 YOS and 20 percent after 30 YOS. Seventy percent of individuals entered this career pattern at GS 1–9, while 23 percent entered at GS 10–12. While most individuals (72 percent) were not promoted beyond GS-12,

Figure 3.4a
Fifty Most Common Career Trajectories: Mid-Grade

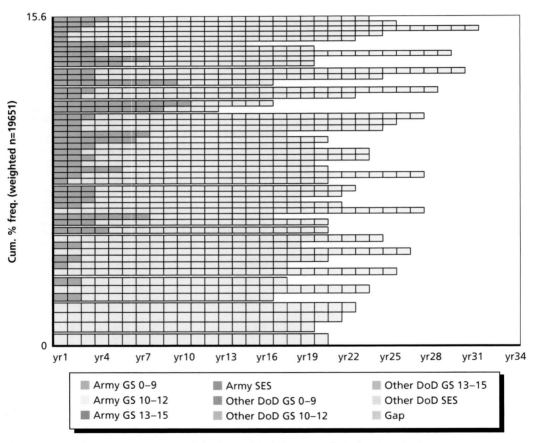

NOTE: Results from one replication of the hierarchical cluster analysis showing the 50 most common career trajectories of individuals identified with the Mid-Grade career pattern. The number of bars, from left to right, indicates the number of years since the individual was first observed, as shown on the horizontal axis. The height of the bar indicates how many individuals share the given trajectory. The "n" in the vertical axis label indicates the total number of individuals assigned to this career pattern in this replication. The percentage shown at the top of the vertical axis indicates the percentage of all unique career trajectories in the career pattern that are captured by the 50 most frequent career trajectories, which are shown in the figure. Authors' calculations based on hierarchical clustering analysis using end-of-year snapshots from the DMDC Civilian Master Files from FY 1980 to FY 2015.
RAND RR2280A-3.4a

Figure 3.4b
Continuation Curve: Mid-Grade

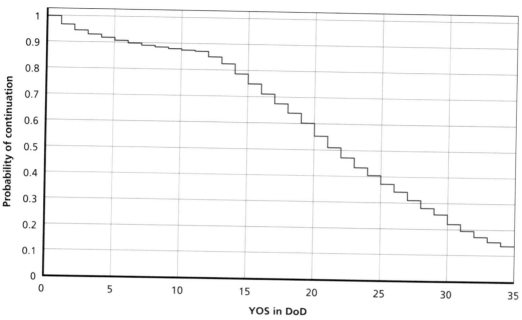

NOTE: Kaplan-Meier estimates of the continuation probabilities after each year of service for employees identified with the Mid-Grade career pattern in the hierarchical cluster analysis. Individuals are identified as departing the first time they are no longer observed in an end-of-FY snapshot, and are observed until the end of FY 2015 or until they leave the DoD civilian workforce. Authors' calculations based on end-of-year snapshots from the DMDC Civilian Master Files from FY 1980 to FY 2015.

RAND RR2280A-3.4b

quite a few (28 percent) were eventually promoted to GS 13–15. About 14 percent of individuals spent some time in other DoD components. About 20 percent of person-years in this career pattern were spent in GS 1–9 in the Army, while 70 percent were spent in GS 10–12 in the Army.

In general, the Mid-Grade career pattern typically includes individuals who entered the Army at relatively low grades, remained in the Army civilian workforce for about 20 years, and were eventually promoted to GS 10–12.

Career Pattern 3: Low-Grade

The Low-Grade career pattern is characterized by long-term service at relatively low grades. Figure 3.5a shows that the top 50 trajectories represent 60 percent of all career trajectories in this career pattern, suggesting a relatively homogeneous set of individual careers. Service of at least 20 years is the norm (Figure 3.5b). Considering all individuals in the clustering analysis as a whole, the probability of continuation after 20 YOS

Figure 3.5a
Fifty Most Common Career Trajectories: Low-Grade

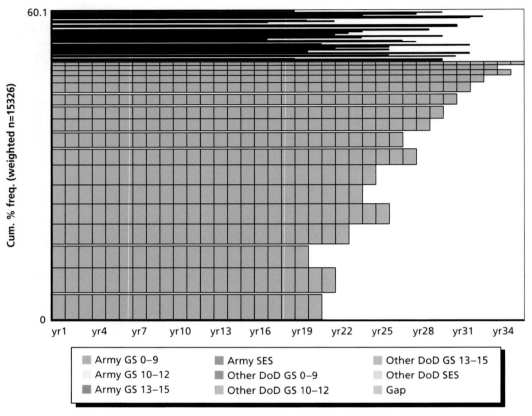

NOTE: Results from one replication of the hierarchical cluster analysis showing the 50 most common career trajectories of individuals identified with the Low-Grade career pattern. The number of bars, from left to right, indicates the number of years since the individual was first observed, as shown on the horizontal axis. The height of the bar indicates how many individuals share the given trajectory. The "n" in the vertical axis label indicates the total number of individuals assigned to this career pattern in this replication. The percentage shown at the top of the vertical axis indicates the percentage of all unique career trajectories in the career pattern that are captured by the 50 most frequent career trajectories, which are shown in the figure. Authors' calculations based on hierarchical clustering analysis using end-of-year snapshots from the DMDC Civilian Master Files from FY 1980 to FY 2015.
RAND *RR2280A-3.5a*

is approximately 20 percent. In contrast, the probability of continuation after 20 YOS is 70 percent for those in the Low-Grade career pattern.

Nearly all of the individuals in this career pattern were initially seen in a relatively low grade (GS 1–9). Some individuals (25 percent) were eventually observed in higher grades (GS 10–12). A number of them (17 percent) were also observed in the civilian workforce in other DoD components at some point, typically in GS 1–9.

Figure 3.5b
Continuation Curve: Low-Grade

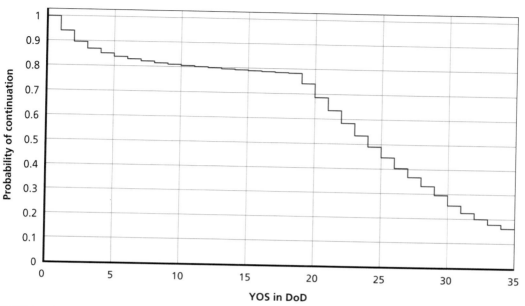

NOTE: Kaplan-Meier estimates of the continuation probabilities after each year of service for employees identified with the Low-Grade career pattern in the hierarchical cluster analysis. Individuals are identified as departing the first time they are no longer observed in an end-of-FY snapshot, and are observed until the end of FY 2015 or until they leave the DoD civilian workforce. Authors' calculations based on end-of-year snapshots from the DMDC Civilian Master Files from FY 1980 to FY 2015.

RAND RR2280A-3.5b

Over 90 percent of the person-years associated with this career pattern were spent in GS 1–9 in the Army.

The Low-Grade career pattern is thus characterized by entry at a relatively low grade, long-term service in the Army civilian workforce, and relatively few promotions beyond GS-9.

Career Pattern 4: High-Grade

Figure 3.6a shows the top 50 career trajectories for the High-Grade career pattern. These trajectories represent only 11.2 percent of all sequences, suggesting substantial heterogeneity in this career pattern. Like the Low-Grade career pattern, the High-Grade career pattern is characterized by long periods of service (Figure 3.6b), albeit with promotion to high grades. The probability of continuation is 75 percent after 20 YOS and 45 percent after 30 YOS.

This career pattern is characterized by substantial career progression. Almost all of the individuals in this career pattern were eventually promoted to GS 13–15.

Figure 3.6a
Fifty Most Common Career Trajectories: High-Grade

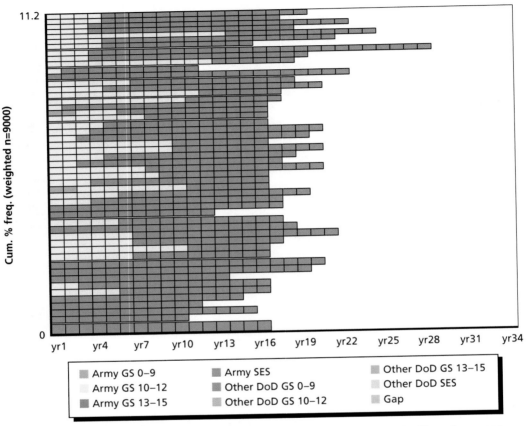

NOTE: Results from one replication of the hierarchical cluster analysis showing the 50 most common career trajectories of individuals identified with the High-Grade career pattern. The number of bars, from left to right, indicates the number of years since the individual was first observed, as shown on the horizontal axis. The height of the bar indicates how many individuals share the given trajectory. The "n" in the vertical axis label indicates the total number of individuals assigned to this career pattern in this replication. The percentage shown at the top of the vertical axis indicates the percentage of all unique career trajectories in the career pattern that are captured by the 50 most frequent career trajectories, which are shown in the figure. Authors' calculations based on hierarchical clustering analysis using end-of-year snapshots from the DMDC Civilian Master Files from FY 1980 to FY 2015.

RAND RR2280A-3.6a

However, nearly 55 percent started at GS 1–9, while 33 percent started at GS 10–12. Considering all of the person-years associated with this career pattern, about 8 percent are in GS 1–9 in the Army, 32 percent are in GS 10–12 in the Army, and 58 percent are in GS 13–15 in the Army. About 12 percent of individuals do spend some time in other DoD components, although this represents a small share (2 percent) of total person-years in this career pattern.

Figure 3.6b
Continuation Curve: High-Grade

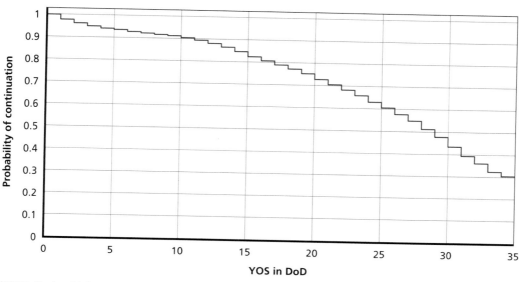

NOTE: Kaplan-Meier estimates of the continuation probabilities after each year of service for employees identified with the High-Grade career pattern in the hierarchical cluster analysis. Individuals are identified as departing the first time they are no longer observed in an end-of-FY snapshot, and are observed until the end of FY 2015 or until they leave the DoD civilian workforce. Authors' calculations based on end-of-year snapshots from the DMDC Civilian Master Files from FY 1980 to FY 2015.
RAND RR2280A-3.6b

On the whole, the High-Grade career pattern is characterized by individuals who spend a long career in the Army civilian workforce and who are promoted through multiple grades during their careers, eventually reaching one of the highest GS levels.

Career Pattern 5: Multiple Components, Low-Grade

The Multiple Components, Low Grade career pattern is characterized by time spent in multiple DoD components at relatively low grades (Figure 3.7a). Like the Mid-Grade and High-Grade career patterns, the Multiple Components, Low-Grade career pattern is heterogeneous, with the top 50 trajectories representing only 15.6 percent of all trajectories.

All individuals in this career pattern spend at least some time in the civilian workforce of a DoD component other than the Army. Figure 3.7b shows the continuation curve for this career pattern. Note that these curves indicate time in all DoD service; the probability of continuation is 70 percent after 10 YOS and 45 percent after 20 YOS. However, although individuals in this career pattern spend, on average, 23 years in the DoD civilian workforce, they are observed in the Army civilian workforce for an average of only 6 years.

Figure 3.7a
Fifty Most Common Career Trajectories: Multiple Components, Low-Grade

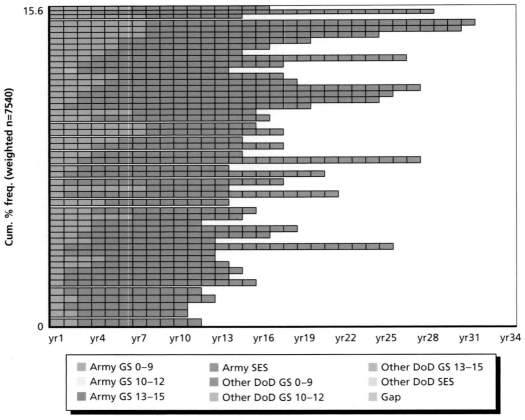

NOTE: Results from one replication of the hierarchical cluster analysis showing the 50 most common career trajectories of individuals identified with the Multiple Components, Low-Grade career pattern. The number of bars, from left to right, indicates the number of years since the individual was first observed, as shown on the horizontal axis. The height of the bar indicates how many individuals share the given trajectory. The "n" in the vertical axis label indicates the total number of individuals assigned to this career pattern in this replication. The percentage shown at the top of the vertical axis indicates the percentage of all unique career trajectories in the career pattern that are captured by the 50 most frequent career trajectories, which are shown in the figure. Authors' calculations based on hierarchical clustering analysis using end-of-year snapshots from the DMDC Civilian Master Files from FY 1980 to FY 2015.

RAND RR2280A-3.7a

Nearly all individuals in this career pattern began in GS 1–9. Sixty-six percent began in the Army, while the others began in another DoD service but later spent time in the Army. About 20 percent were eventually promoted beyond GS-9, and 3 percent were promoted beyond GS-12. Considering the total number of person-years in this career pattern, the majority (75 percent) was spent in a DoD service other than the Army.

Figure 3.7b
Continuation Curve: Multiple Components, Low-Grade

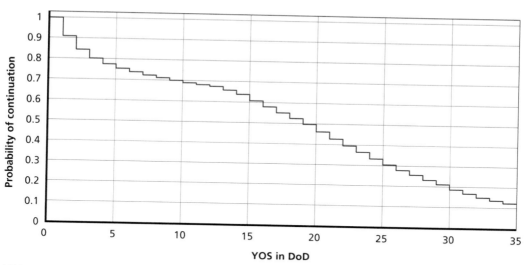

NOTE: Kaplan-Meier estimates of the continuation probabilities after each year of service for employees identified with the Multiple Components, Low-Grade career pattern in the hierarchical cluster analysis. Individuals are identified as departing the first time they are no longer observed in an end-of-FY snapshot, and are observed until the end of FY 2015 or until they leave the DoD civilian workforce. Authors' calculations based on end-of-year snapshots from the DMDC Civilian Master Files from FY 1980 to FY 2015.

RAND RR2280A-3.7b

Overall, the Multiple Components, Low-Grade career pattern represents long-term service in the DoD civilian workforce, generally at low grades, with a relatively small share of that time spent in the Army.

Career Pattern 6: Multiple Components, Higher Grades

The Multiple Components, Higher Grades career pattern is the most heterogeneous of the patterns we identify, with the top 50 trajectories representing only 2.5 percent of all trajectories (Figure 3.8a). Like the individuals in the Multiple Components, Low-Grade pattern, all individuals in the Multiple Components, Higher Grades career pattern spent at least some time in another part of the DoD civilian work-force. Also like the Multiple Components, Low-Grade pattern, while the probabil-ity of continuation in the DoD civilian workforce is approximately 60 percent after 20 YOS (Figure 3.8b), individuals in this pattern are only observed in the Army civilian workforce for an average of 7 years. Considering the total number of person-years in this career pattern, the majority (75 percent) was spent in a DoD service other than the Army.

What distinguishes this career pattern from the previous one is grade progres-sion. Although approximately 60 percent of individuals in this career pattern started at

Figure 3.8a
Fifty Most Common Career Trajectories: Multiple Components, Higher Grades

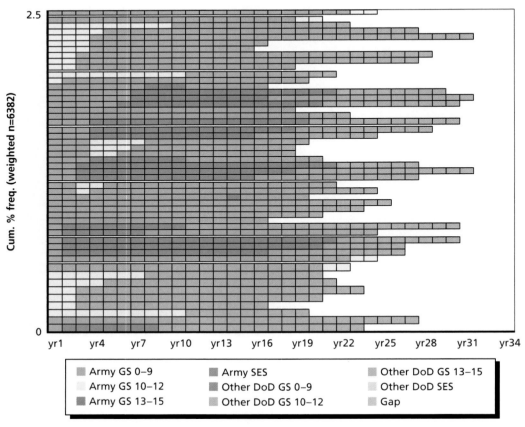

NOTE: Results from one replication of the hierarchical cluster analysis showing the 50 most common career trajectories of individuals identified with the Multiple Components, Higher Grades career pattern. The number of bars, from left to right, indicates the number of years since the individual was first observed, as shown on the horizontal axis. The height of the bar indicates how many individuals share the given trajectory. The "n" in the vertical axis label indicates the total number of individuals assigned to this career pattern in this replication. The percentage shown at the top of the vertical axis indicates the percentage of all unique career trajectories in the career pattern that are captured by the 50 most frequent career trajectories, which are shown in the figure. Authors' calculations based on hierarchical clustering analysis using end-of-year snapshots from the DMDC Civilian Master Files from FY 1980 to FY 2015.

RAND RR2280A-3.8a

GS 1–9, all of them were eventually promoted to GS-10 or above, and 50 percent were promoted to GS-13 or above.

Much like the Mid-Grade and High-Grade career patterns, the Multiple Components, Higher Grades pattern is characterized by long-term service and career progression within the DoD civilian workforce as a whole.

Figure 3.8b
Continuation Curve: Multiple Components, Higher Grades

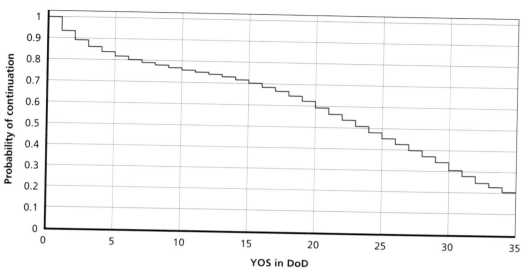

NOTE: Kaplan-Meier estimates of the continuation probabilities after each year of service for employees identified with the Multiple Components, Higher Grades career pattern in the hierarchical cluster analysis. Individuals are identified as departing the first time they are no longer observed in an end-of-FY snapshot, and are observed until the end of FY 2015 or until they leave the DoD civilian workforce. Authors' calculations based on end-of-year snapshots from the DMDC Civilian Master Files from FY 1980 to FY 2015.
RAND RR2280A-3.8b

Career Pattern 7: Long Gap

The Long Gap career pattern includes a number of individuals who began their careers in the Army, left the DoD civilian workforce altogether, and later returned. Ninety-five percent of the individuals in this career pattern have a gap of at least five years, and 66 percent have a gap of more than 15 years. This career pattern is heterogeneous, with the top 50 trajectories representing only 5 percent of all trajectories (Figure 3.9a).

Figure 3.9b shows the continuation curve until the first time leaving the DoD civilian workforce. The probability of continuation is 30 percent at five YOS and only 10 percent at 10 YOS. Over 50 percent spend some time in another DoD service; however, 70 percent of total person-years in the DoD civilian workforce are spent in the Army. Nearly all individuals in this career pattern enter in GS 1–9. About 60 percent are eventually promoted to GS-10 or above, and nearly 20 percent are promoted to GS-13 or above.

Overall, the Long Gap career pattern is characterized by individuals who exhibit a long stretch between periods of service in the DoD civilian workforce. Unfortunately, given the limitations of the DMDC data, it is not practical to track what these

Figure 3.9a
Fifty Most Common Career Trajectories: Long Gap

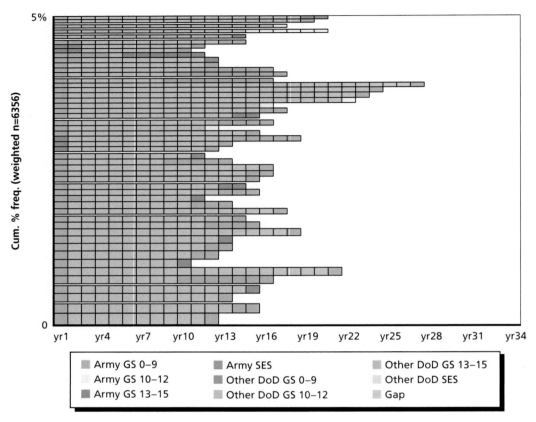

NOTE: Results from one replication of the hierarchical cluster analysis showing the 50 most common career trajectories of individuals identified with the Long Gap career pattern. The number of bars, from left to right, indicates the number of years since the individual was first observed, as shown on the horizontal axis. The height of the bar indicates how many individuals share the given trajectory. The "n" in the vertical axis label indicates the total number of individuals assigned to this career pattern in this replication. The percentage shown at the top of the vertical axis indicates the percentage of all unique career trajectories in the career pattern that are captured by the 50 most frequent career trajectories, which are shown in the figure. Authors' calculations based on hierarchical clustering analysis using end-of-year snapshots from the DMDC Civilian Master Files from FY 1980 to FY 2015.
RAND RR2280A-3.9a

individuals were doing during their absences. If they were gaining additional years of experience either in another federal agency or in the private sector, then it is not surprising that a sizable share is eventually promoted to relatively high GS grades.

The Role of Entry Cohorts
The continuation curves above showed that there are some differences between the various entry cohorts used in our analysis. We limited the analysis to only the FY 1981–2000 cohorts to allow us to observe career trajectories for at least 15 years.

Figure 3.9b
Continuation Curve: Long Gap

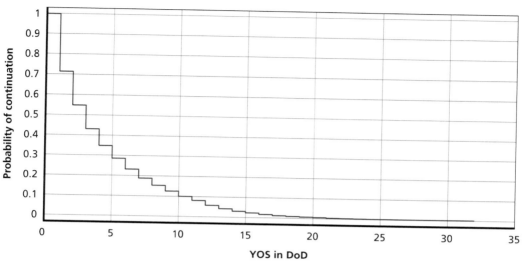

NOTE: Kaplan-Meier estimates of the continuation probabilities after each year of service for employees identified with the Long Gap career pattern in the hierarchical cluster analysis. Individuals are identified as departing the first time they are no longer observed in an end-of-FY snapshot, and are observed until the end of FY 2015 or until they leave the DoD civilian workforce. Authors' calculations based on end-of-year snapshots from the DMDC Civilian Master Files from FY 1980 to FY 2015.
RAND RR2280A-3.9b

However, given that many individuals remain in service for more than 15 years, the distribution of career patterns is likely to vary by entry cohort. In particular, the OM method may be less likely to classify individuals in later entry cohorts into the longer-term career patterns, simply because we observe them for fewer years.

Figure 3.10 shows the distribution of career patterns by entry cohort. In general, the distribution of career patterns is stable across entry cohorts. However, in the most recent entry cohorts, the share of individuals classified in the Short-Term career pattern rises slightly, as does the share in the Mid-Grade career pattern, while the share in the Low-Grade career pattern falls to zero. This is likely because we cannot observe these individuals for more than 15 to 20 years, and most individuals in the Low-Grade career pattern remained in service for at least 20 years.

We further explore the differences across cohorts in Table 3.2, which compares the mean and median lengths of service associated with each career pattern, by five-year entry cohort. The mean and median lengths of service for the Short-Term career pattern are similar across all cohorts. However, for career patterns characterized by longer lengths of service, both mean and median lengths of service are somewhat lower in the later entry cohort groups.

These findings suggest a potential concern that the cluster analysis assigns individuals who would have been in the longer-term career patterns if they could have been

Figure 3.10
Distribution of Career Patterns by Entry Cohort

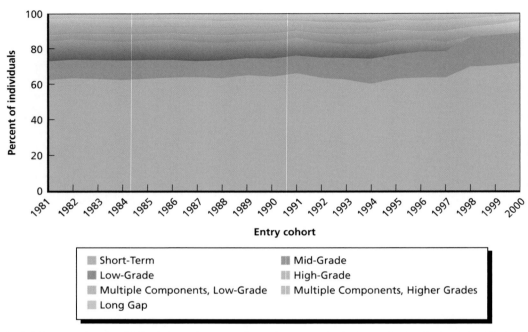

NOTE: Percentage of individuals in each entry cohort shown on the horizontal axis who are identified with each career pattern. Authors' calculations based on hierarchical clustering analysis using end-of-year snapshots from the DMDC Civilian Master Files from FY 1980 to FY 2015.

RAND RR2280A-3.10

Table 3.2
YOS by Career Pattern and Entry Cohort

Career Pattern	FY 1981–1985		FY 1986–1990		FY 1991–1995		FY 1996–2000	
	Mean	Median	Mean	Median	Mean	Median	Mean	Median
Short-Term	6.6	5	6.0	5	5.6	4	7.4	6
Mid-Grade	23.7	24	22.6	23	20.2	21	16.7	17
Low-Grade	26.6	27	25.0	26	22.2	22	19.4	19
High-Grade	27.8	30	25.2	27	21.4	22	16.8	17
Multiple Components, Low-Grade	24.2	24	23.1	24	20.6	21	16.7	17
Multiple Components, Higher Grades	27.1	28	25.0	26	21.1	22	17.1	17
Long Gap	12.7	12	11.4	11	9.9	10	7.2	7

NOTE: Mean and median years for which individuals in each career pattern were observed in the DoD civilian workforce, by entry cohort. Authors' calculations based on hierarchical clustering analysis using end-of-year snapshots from the DMDC Civilian Master Files from FY 1980 to FY 2015.

observed for longer periods of time, to other career patterns. This concern is likely to be greater for more recent cohorts. As shown in Table 3.3, among the 180,000 individuals in our sample, 17 percent were still on board at the end of FY 2015; in other words, their careers were censored. The share of entrants whose careers are censored increases from less than 10 percent for the earliest cohorts to 35 percent or more for the FY 1997–2000 cohorts.

Table 3.3
Individuals Still on Board in FY 2015, by Entry Cohort

Entry Year	Number Still on Board	Total	Percent Still on Board
1981	1,205	16,054	8
1982	1,208	15,004	8
1983	1,352	13,936	10
1984	1,865	15,859	12
1985	2,357	17,486	13
1986	1,774	12,477	14
1987	1,994	12,997	15
1988	1,595	8,954	18
1989	2,352	12,810	18
1990	1,340	6,833	20
1991	1,751	8,911	20
1992	1,403	6,190	23
1993	999	4,006	25
1994	1,130	4,037	28
1995	1,305	4,555	29
1996	1,231	3,945	31
1997	1,120	3,203	35
1998	1,304	3,478	37
1999	1,650	4,142	40
2000	2,107	5,123	41
Total	31,042	180,000	17

NOTE: Number and share of individuals in each entry cohort who were observed in the DoD civilian workforce at the end of FY 2015. Authors' calculations based on end-of-year snapshots from the DMDC Civilian Master Files from FY 1980 to FY 2015.

Table 3.4
Career Patterns Excluding FY 1997–2000 Cohorts

Career Pattern	Percent, FY 1981–2000	Percent, FY 1981–1996
Short-Term	64.4	62.9
Mid-Grade	11.0	9.0
Low-Grade	9.5	14.3
High-Grade	4.1	2.6
Multiple Components, Low-Grade	3.9	5.4
Multiple Components, Higher Grades	3.8	2.8
Long Gap	3.3	3.0

NOTE: Percentage of individual career trajectories identified with each career pattern. The second column replicates the original results from Table 3.1. The third column shows results from one hierarchical clustering run using only individuals who entered between FY 1981 and FY 1996. Authors' calculations based on hierarchical clustering analysis using end-of-year snapshots from the DMDC Civilian Master Files from FY 1980 to FY 2015.

To investigate the extent of this concern, we conducted one instance of the hierarchical clustering analysis including only the FY 1981–1996 cohorts. We used FY 1996 as the latest cohort because we can observe up to 20 YOS for this cohort, and because one-third or more of the individual careers in later cohorts are censored (Table 3.3).

Table 3.4 shows the share of individual career trajectories in each career pattern based on the original analysis (reproduced from Table 3.1). In addition, it shows the share of individual career trajectories in each career pattern based on the analysis that includes only FY 1981–1996.[7] The share of individual careers classified as Short-Term falls slightly, from 64.4 percent to 62.9 percent, in the analysis that excludes the most recent cohorts. At the same time, the share of careers classified as Low-Grade rises from 9.5 percent to 14.3 percent, while the shares of Mid-Grade and High-Grade career patterns fall slightly. Overall, however, the same general pattern holds: short-term service remains the most common pattern, followed by relatively long-term service in the Army at various grades, and then by more varied patterns including service in other parts of DoD, and gaps.

---

[7] The FY 1981–2000 shares are based on the modal values from 50 replications, as described in Chapter Two. The FY 1981–1996 shares are based on only one pattern analysis.

CHAPTER FOUR

Career Patterns and Individual and Job Characteristics

In this chapter, we examine the extent to which membership in the career patterns identified in Chapter Three is associated with demographic and job characteristics. For brevity, we focus on three characteristics: gender, prior military service, and career program at entry. Appendix C contains summary statistics for the characteristics among individuals in the sample, and Appendix D contains results for a number of additional characteristics.

For each characteristic, we first show continuation curves by the characteristic in question. We then show the distribution of career patterns by each characteristic. For example, we show the distribution of career patterns for women and men.

The difference in career pattern membership for each characteristic may be driven by differences in other observable characteristics. For example, the difference in distribution by gender may be due in part to the different education levels and occupational choices of men and women. As described in Chapter Two, we estimate a multinomial logistic regression model of the probability of being classified in each career pattern, as a function of a variety of individual and job characteristics. We then estimate the marginal effect of each characteristic on the probability of being classified in each career pattern, controlling for the other observable characteristics.

For differences by gender, we also present results from Oaxaca-Blinder decompositions of the relationship between career pattern and gender. These decompositions allow us to identify the extent to which the differences in career pattern membership by gender may be "explained" by other observable characteristics.

Gender

Figure 4.1a shows continuation curves for all individuals in the cluster analysis, for men and women separately. In this figure, as in the subsequent continuation curves, we do not show confidence intervals, as they are very small and difficult to discern visually. However, a log-rank test finds that the curves are statistically different for men and women ($p < .0001$). Continuation probabilities for women are lower for almost all YOS. After five YOS, the probability of continuation is about 65 percent for men, but

Figure 4.1a
Continuation Curves by Gender

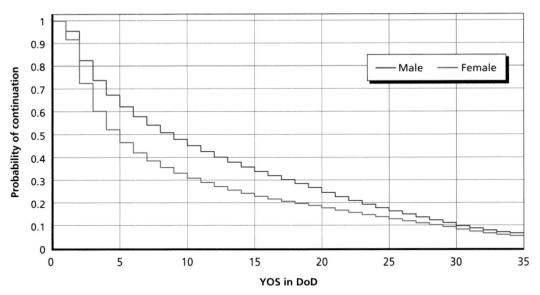

YOS in DoD

NOTE: Kaplan-Meier estimates, by gender, of the continuation probabilities after each year of service for employees in the hierarchical cluster analysis. Individuals are identified as departing the first time they are no longer observed in an end-of-FY snapshot, and are observed until the end of FY 2015 or until they leave the DoD civilian workforce. Authors' calculations based on end-of-year snapshots from the DMDC Civilian Master Files from FY 1980 to FY 2015.

RAND RR2280A-4.1a

less than 50 percent for women; after 10 YOS, the probabilities are about 45 percent and 30 percent, respectively. In later YOS, the gap narrows, and by 30 YOS continuation probabilities are fairly similar, as few men or women remain.

In keeping with these continuation rates, Figure 4.1b shows that nearly 68 percent of women, but only 59 percent of men, are in the Short-Term career pattern. Figure 4.1b also shows that women are also more likely to be in the Low-Grade career pattern, whereas men are more likely to be in the Mid-Grade and High-Grade career patterns.

In Figure 4.1c, we show the marginal effects of being female on the probability of being in each career pattern—in other words, we show the effects of gender on career pattern membership, after controlling for a variety of other observable characteristics. The magnitude of the bars can be interpreted as the percentage point difference in probability of career pattern membership for women, relative to men.

Consider the Short-Term career pattern. In Figure 4.1b, the raw results indicated that women were about 9 percentage points more likely to be classified in the Short-Term career pattern than men (see the difference between men and women in the length of the blue bars in Figure 4.1b). Figure 4.1c shows that, after controlling for

Figure 4.1b
Distribution of Career Patterns by Gender

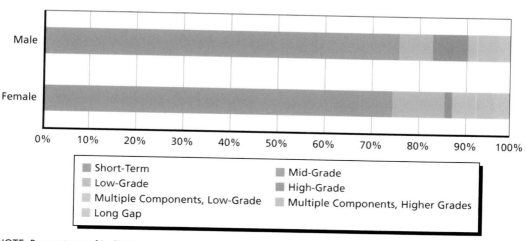

NOTE: Percentage of individual career trajectories identified with each career pattern, by gender. Authors' calculations based on hierarchical clustering analysis using end-of-year snapshots from the DMDC Civilian Master Files from FY 1980 to FY 2015.

RAND RR2280A-4.1b

Figure 4.1c
Marginal Effects of Being a Female on Career Pattern (Relative to Males)

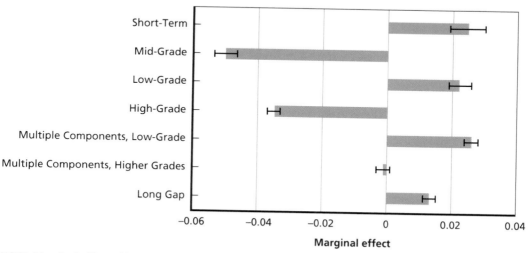

NOTE: Marginal effect of being female on probability of being in each career pattern. Results are based on a multinomial logistic regression of the probability of being in each career pattern, and can be interpreted as the percentage point difference in probability of career pattern membership, relative to men. Black bars indicate 95 percent confidence intervals. Authors' calculations based on hierarchical clustering and regression analysis using end-of-year snapshots from the DMDC Civilian Master Files from FY 1980 to FY 2015.

RAND RR2280A-4.1c

the observable characteristics listed earlier, women are only 2.5 percentage points more likely to be classified in this career pattern. In other words, if about 60 percent of men are in the Short-Term career pattern, then we would expect 62.5 percent of women to be in this career pattern. The reason that the percentage point difference is lower after controlling for other factors is that the women in the sample are more likely to exhibit other characteristics that are also associated with being in the Short-Term pattern. For example, as we show in Appendix D, individuals who are hired on temporary or term appointments are more likely than those hired on career or career conditional appointments to be in the Short-Term career pattern. Women are more likely to be hired on temporary or term appointments, so controlling for the type of appointment accounts for some of the raw difference between men and women.

Referring again to Figure 4.1c, women are also more likely to be in a low-grade career pattern (Low-Grade; Multiple Components, Low-Grade) or in the Long Gap pattern, and less likely to be in the mid- to high-grade patterns.

As illustrated by the differences between Figures 4.1b and 4.1c, some part of the differences in career pattern by gender can be "explained" based on other observable characteristics. Next, we use the Oaxaca-Blinder decomposition method to more explicitly identify what share of the difference can be "explained," and by which characteristics.

Figure 4.2a shows the initial decomposition of the difference in career pattern membership into "explained" and "unexplained" components. In general, the total length of each bar in Figure 4.2a is equal to the raw difference between the percentage of women and the percentage of men in each career pattern, as shown in Figure 4.1b. For example, Figure 4.1b indicates that women are about 9 percentage points more likely than men to be in the Short-Term career pattern. This 9-percentage-point difference can be decomposed into what is explainable by the other observable variables (red) and unexplainable by those same variables (blue) as shown in the top bar in Figure 4.2a.

Each of the bars in Figure 4.2a similarly decomposes the explainable and unexplainable portions for each career pattern. For example, women are about 10 percentage points less likely than men to be in the Mid-Grade pattern (see Figure 4.1b). Figure 4.2a shows the proportions of that difference that are explainable and unexplainable in the second bar from the top.

In the case of the Long Gap pattern, the other observable characteristics suggest that women should be less likely to be in this pattern; that is, the length of the "explained" bar is −0.01. In reality, though, women are more likely to be observed in this pattern. Hence, the length of the "unexplained" bar is +0.02. The sum of these two bars (−0.01 + 0.02) is 0.01, which is the raw difference shown in Figure 4.1b.

The decomposition shown in Figure 4.2a includes the observed characteristics listed in Chapter Two, including career program at entry. We also performed a decomposition using each individual's four-digit occupational code at entry, instead of career

Figure 4.2a
Decomposition of Differences in Career Pattern by Gender

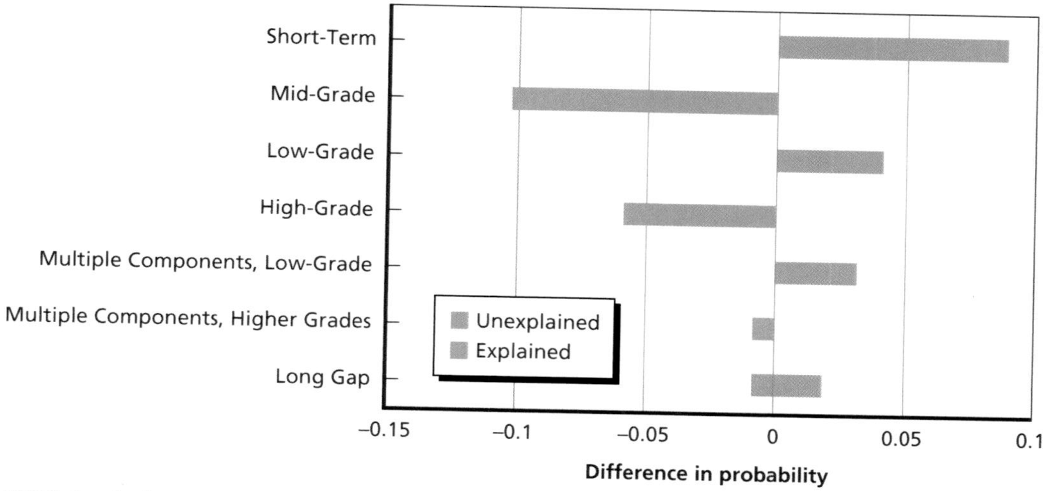

NOTE: Results from Oaxaca-Blinder decompositions of the "explained" and "unexplained" components associated with the difference in probability that women are observed in each career pattern, relative to men. Authors' calculations based on hierarchical clustering and decomposition analysis using end-of-year snapshots from the DMDC Civilian Master Files from FY 1980 to FY 2015.
RAND RR2280A-4.2a

program, for two reasons. First, as noted in Chapter Two, to create a one-to-one concordance between occupational codes and career programs, we had to group several career programs together, so our measure of career program at entry may include a number of dissimilar occupations. Second, career programs were not in place for many individuals for much of the time period we consider, so occupation may have more predictive power.

Figure 4.2b confirms that using occupation at entry does, in fact, explain a larger share of the difference in career pattern membership by gender. In fact, the entire difference in Short-Term career pattern membership is explained by the combination of observable characteristics.

To understand in greater detail which of these other characteristics account for the observed differences, we break down the explained portion of career pattern membership into specific observable characteristics (Figure 4.3). We present the decomposition that relies on occupation at entry, rather than career program at entry, since occupation at entry explains a larger share of the differences. In Figure 4.3, the length of the bar for each pattern may be slightly different from the length in Figure 4.2b. This is because certain characteristics are associated with an increase in the probability that women are observed in a particular career pattern, while others are associated with a decrease. The sum of increases plus decreases will be equal to the overall share of the probability that is "explained" as shown in Figure 4.2b.

Figure 4.2b
Decomposition of Differences in Career Pattern by Gender, Controlling for Occupation at Entry

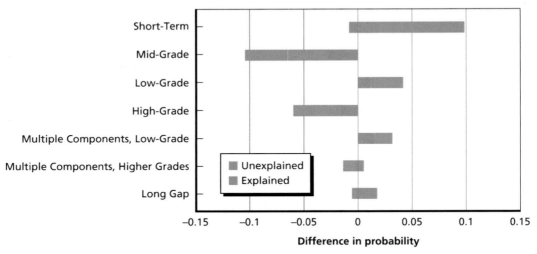

NOTE: Results from Oaxaca-Blinder decompositions of the "explained" and "unexplained" components associated with the difference in probability that women are observed in each career pattern, relative to men. The decomposition includes occupation at entry rather than career program group at entry. Authors' calculations based on hierarchical clustering and decomposition analysis using end-of-year snapshots from the DMDC Civilian Master Files from FY 1980 to FY 2015.
RAND *RR2280A-4.2b*

For example, in the Short-Term pattern, occupation at entry "explains" 5.4 percentage points of the difference between men and women. In other words, women tend to enter occupations that are associated with shorter lengths of service. In addition, prior military service "explains" 4.9 percentage points of the increase in probability that women are in this career pattern. The likely reason is that lack of prior service is associated with a higher probability of being in the Short-Term career pattern, and women are less likely to have prior service.

Similarly, the fact that career appointments are associated with a lower probability of being in this career pattern, and that women are less likely to enter with career appointments, explains about 1.8 percentage points of the increase. Education at entry explains 0.5 percentage points of the difference.

Offsetting these increases are decreases in the probability of membership in this career pattern, explained by age at entry (negative 2.3 percentage points) and a combination of all other observables that we included (negative 0.6 percentage points in total). Overall, these changes add up to 9.6 percentage points, the "explained" share of the difference from Figure 4.2b.

In general, of all the characteristics we observe, prior military service and occupation at entry play the largest roles in explaining the differences in career pattern

Figure 4.3
Decomposition of Differences in Career Pattern by Gender, "Explained" Portion

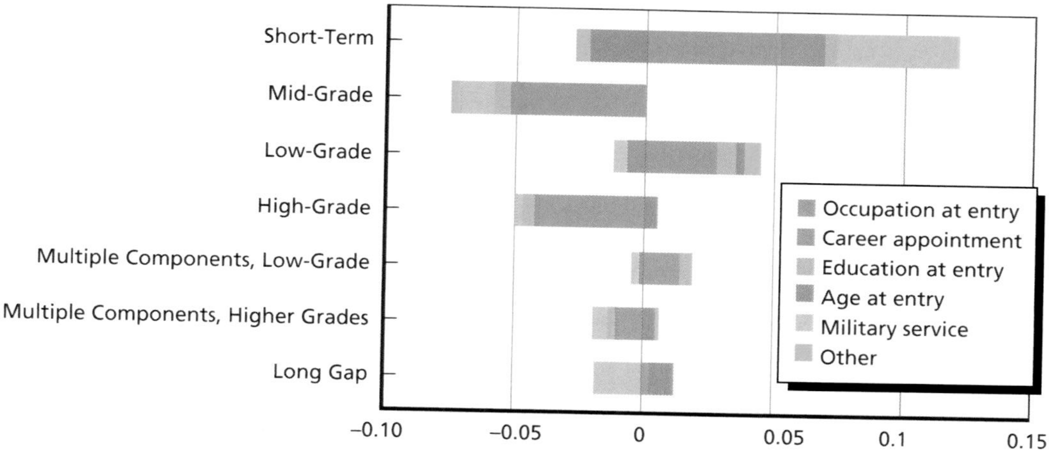

NOTE: Results from detailed Oaxaca-Blinder decompositions of the "explained" components associated with the difference in probability that women are observed in each career pattern, relative to men. The decomposition includes occupation at entry rather than career program group at entry. Authors' calculations based on hierarchical clustering and decomposition analysis using end-of-year snapshots from the DMDC Civilian Master Files from FY 1980 to FY 2015.
RAND RR2280A-4.3

membership for men and women. To the extent that women make up a higher share of entrants into occupations that do not offer as much scope for advancement, such as administrative roles, this occupational selection may be reflected in future career patterns. To a much greater degree than men, women tend to fall into the group of employees whom we describe as short-term.

Prior Military Service

Figure 4.4a shows continuation curves for nonveterans, veterans who are not identified as military retirees, and military retirees.[1] During the first 20 YOS, continuation probabilities for nonretired veterans are slightly higher than continuation probabilities for nonveterans. Continuation rates for military retirees are even higher; after 10 YOS, the probability of continuation is approximately 60 percent for military retirees, compared with 40 percent for nonretired veterans and 35 percent for nonveterans. This pattern

---

[1]   A log-rank test finds that the curves are statistically different across these groups ($p < .0001$).

Figure 4.4a
Continuation Curves by Prior Military Service

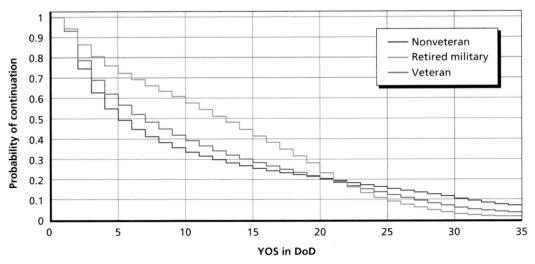

NOTE: Kaplan-Meier estimates, by prior military service, of the continuation probabilities after each year of service for employees in the hierarchical cluster analysis. Individuals are identified as departing the first time they are no longer observed in an end-of-FY snapshot, and are observed until the end of FY 2015 or until they leave the DoD civilian workforce. Authors' calculations based on end-of-year snapshots from the DMDC Civilian Master Files from FY 1980 to FY 2015.
RAND RR2280A-4.4a

reverses after 20 YOS, with nonveterans more likely to remain than nonretired veterans, and military retirees least likely to remain.

Figures 4.4b and 4.4c show the distribution of individuals across career patterns by veteran status. In Figure 4.4c, the magnitude of the bars can be interpreted as the percentage point difference in probability of career pattern membership for nonretired veterans and military retirees, relative to nonveterans.

After controlling for observable characteristics, nonretired veterans are about 3 percentage points less likely to appear in the Short-Term pattern, while military retirees are 29 percentage points less likely to do so. Military retirees are also more likely to appear in the Mid-Grade pattern. Nonretired veterans are approximately as likely as nonveterans to be in the Low-Grade pattern, and are less likely to be in the High-Grade pattern; in contrast, military retirees are more likely to be in both the Low-Grade and High-Grade patterns. Both nonretired veterans and military retirees are more likely to spend time in other DoD services and to exhibit a gap in service.

Taken together, the results suggest that veterans, and particularly military retirees, who join the DoD civilian workforce are less likely to leave DoD completely after a short period of time, but are also more likely to be mobile across DoD components and to have a gap in service.

Figure 4.4b
Distribution of Career Patterns by Prior Military Service

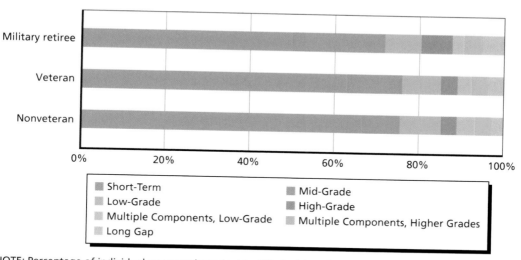

NOTE: Percentage of individual career trajectories identified with each career pattern, by prior military service. Authors' calculations based on hierarchical clustering analysis using end-of-year snapshots from the DMDC Civilian Master Files from FY 1980 to FY 2015.
RAND RR2280A-4.4b

Figure 4.4c
Marginal Effects of Prior Military Service on Career Pattern (Relative to Nonveterans)

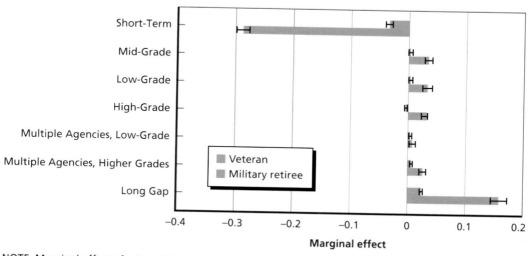

NOTE: Marginal effect of prior military service on probability of being in each career pattern. Results are based on a multinomial logistic regression of the probability of being in each career pattern, and can be interpreted as the percentage point difference in probability of career pattern membership, relative to nonveterans. Black bars indicate 95 percent confidence intervals. Authors' calculations based on hierarchical clustering and regression analysis using end-of-year snapshots from the DMDC Civilian Master Files from FY 1980 to FY 2015.
RAND RR2280A-4.4c

Career Program at Entry

Figure 4.5a shows continuation curves for the five largest career program groups.[2] As discussed in Chapter Two, we mapped occupations into career programs and, in certain cases, had to group career programs together to form a unique concordance between occupations and career programs. Because individuals can switch career programs as they move between positions, we classified individuals based on career program at entry.

Relative to the largest group—Administration, Management, and Legal—continuation probabilities are slightly higher for Comptroller, IT and Modeling, and Engineering, Science, and Medical; probabilities are similar for Supply Management.

Figures 4.5b and 4.5c show the distribution of individuals across career patterns by career program at entry. In Figure 4.5c, the magnitude of the bars can be interpreted as the percentage point difference in probability of career pattern membership

Figure 4.5a
Continuation Curves by Career Program

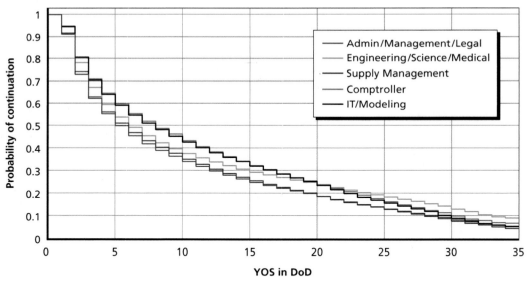

NOTE: Kaplan-Meier estimates, by career program group associated with initial occupation, of the continuation probabilities after each year of service for employees in the hierarchical cluster analysis. Individuals are identified as departing the first time they are no longer observed in an end-of-FY snapshot, and are observed until the end of FY 2015 or until they leave the DoD civilian workforce. Authors' calculations based on end-of-year snapshots from the DMDC Civilian Master Files from FY 1980 to FY 2015.

RAND RR2280A-4.5a

---

[2] A log-rank test finds that the curves are statistically different across these five career program groups ($p < .0001$).

Figure 4.5b
Distribution of Career Patterns by Career Program

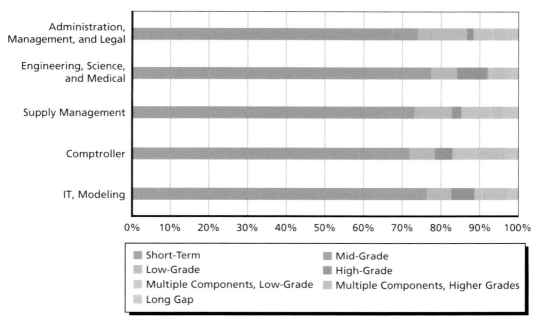

NOTE: Percentage of individual career trajectories identified with each career pattern, by career program group associated with initial occupation. Authors' calculations based on hierarchical clustering analysis using end-of-year snapshots from the DMDC Civilian Master Files from FY 1980 to FY 2015.
RAND *RR2280A-4.5b*

for the specific career program, relative to the Administration, Management, and Legal career program.

After controlling for observable characteristics, those who enter the Comptroller, IT and Modeling, and Supply Management groups are less likely to be in the Short-Term career pattern, relative to those in the Administration, Management, and Legal group.[3] These three groups exhibit similar propensities to be in the career patterns in which service is concentrated in the Army civilian workforce, but exhibit different propensities to be in the career patterns associated with service in other parts of DoD. The Comptroller group is more likely to serve in other parts of DoD at both lower and higher grades, the Supply Management group is more likely to serve in other parts of DoD only in low grades, and the IT and Modeling group is more likely to serve in other parts of DoD in higher grades.

Those in the Engineering, Science, and Medical group are more likely to serve in the Army in mid- and high grades, and less likely to move to other parts of DoD at any grade.

---

[3]   The full set of regression results, including all career programs, is shown in Appendix D.

Figure 4.5c
Marginal Effects of Career Program on Career Pattern (Relative to Those Initially in the Administration, Management, and Legal Career Program Group)

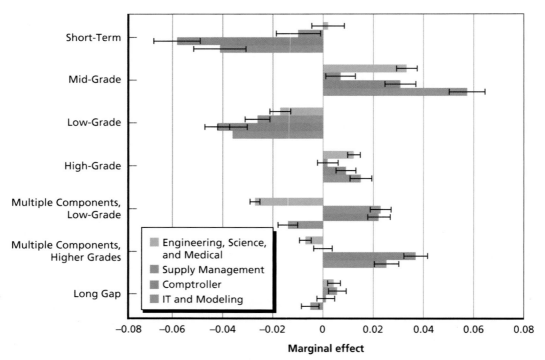

NOTE: Marginal effect of career program group associated with initial occupation on probability of being in each career pattern. Results are based on a multinomial logistic regression of the probability of being in each career pattern, and can be interpreted as the percentage point difference in probability of career pattern membership, relative to individuals who were initially observed in occupations associated with the Administration, Management, and Legal career program group. Black bars indicate 95 percent confidence intervals. Authors' calculations based on hierarchical clustering and regression analysis using end-of-year snapshots from the DMDC Civilian Master Files from FY 1980 to FY 2015.

RAND *RR2280A-4.5c*

CHAPTER FIVE
Conclusions

In this chapter, we summarize key findings from our analyses and discuss potential implications for Army civilian workforce managers.

Key Findings

Army civilians exhibit a diverse array of career trajectories, and most entrants into the Army civilian workforce spend a relatively short amount of time there. Nearly two-thirds of all individuals in the cluster analysis were identified with the Short-Term career pattern, characterized by few years spent in the Army civilian workforce (and the DoD civilian workforce more generally). If we consider all individuals in the cluster analysis (not just those identified with the Short-Term career pattern), about 40 percent spent five or fewer years in the DoD civilian workforce. Since our sample was limited to those who spent at least two years in service, that share is even higher if we consider all individuals who spent time in the Army civilian workforce, in the GS, SES, or NSPS pay plans: about 50 percent of these individuals spent five or fewer years in the DoD civilian workforce. Even restricting the sample to those initially hired on a career or career conditional appointment only reduces the share to about 40 percent.

Of course, since employees who remain for longer periods of time contribute more years of service to the Army and DoD civilian workforces, the share of person-years of service contributed by short-term employees is not as high as the share of entrants that they represent. Among all individuals who spent time in the Army civilian workforce, in the GS, SES, or NSPS pay plans, employees who spent five or fewer years in the DoD civilian workforce contributed only 11 percent of total person-years observed. Nonetheless, it is important for career program managers to understand that most incoming Army civilians are unlikely to spend long periods of time in the Army, or in the DoD civilian workforce more generally.

Career patterns are related to a variety of individual and job characteristics. Women are more likely to be in career patterns that include short-term service, service in low grades, and a long gap in service. The difference between men and women along other dimensions accounts for some part of these differences. Women tend to

51

be hired in occupations that are associated with shorter duration of service and lower grades. In addition, veterans are less likely to exhibit short-term service; since women are less likely than men to be veterans, prior military status may account for some part of the gender differences. However, a substantial share of the differences between male and female career pattern groupings, particularly with respect to long gaps in service, remains unexplained by the factors that we can observe in the data. One key factor that we do not observe is family status, which may explain some of these differences.

As we show in Chapter Four and in Appendix D, career pattern also varies across other demographic characteristics, including race and ethnicity, age and education at entry, and veteran status. Black and Hispanic individuals are more likely to be in one of the Low-Grade career patterns and less likely to be in the higher grade patterns, relative to white individuals. Asians are also more likely to be in the Low-Grade pattern and to spend time in other parts of DoD, at various grade levels. Asians and Hispanics are also less likely to be in the Short-Term pattern.

The youngest and oldest entrants into the DoD civilian workforce are more likely to be in the Short-Term pattern. However, young entrants are also more likely to be in career patterns characterized by eventual promotion to the highest grades, in the Army as well as in other parts of DoD. More educated individuals are more likely to be found in higher-grade patterns, which is consistent with higher educational requirements for positions at higher pay grades. Individuals with prior military service, particularly military retirees, are much less likely to be in the Short-Term pattern. They are also more likely to be mobile across DoD components and to exhibit a gap in service.

The characteristics of an individual's first position are also associated with career pattern. As we would expect, individuals who are initially hired with temporary or term appointments are substantially more likely to be in the Short-Term career pattern and less likely to be in any of the patterns associated with long-term Army or DoD service. There is some variation in career pattern across entry cohorts, with individuals in later cohorts more likely to be in the higher-grade career patterns. This finding may be driven by the increase in average GS grade levels in the DoD civilian workforce over time. Career program at entry is also associated with different likelihood of association with different patterns.

Potential Implications for Managing the Army Civilian Workforce

All of the analyses in this report are descriptive—that is, we cannot identify the causal impact of individual characteristics on career pattern. Nonetheless, the findings above suggest a few steps that Army workforce managers may wish to take to better understand the drivers behind these findings, and that may help strengthen the leadership pipeline.

Collect systematic information about why employees leave the Army civilian workforce. Employees who leave the Army civilian workforce should be asked to complete a short exit survey. The survey could be offered to all who leave or targeted to those who leave during a specific time period. This survey should include, at a minimum, questions about the main reasons for leaving the Army civilian workforce. It would also be valuable to identify whether the employee has secured another job and, if so, some basic details about the new job, including location, whether the job is in the private or public sector, and the name of the federal agency (if public) or the industry (if private).

Understanding why employees leave can help Army workforce managers determine whether the high rate of departure during the first few years is a concern. On one hand, spending a relatively short amount of time with an employer is common in today's labor market; the Bureau of Labor Statistics (2016) reports that the average time spent with a current employer among wage and salary workers is 4.2 years. On the other hand, the exit survey may identify specific reasons for departure that Army workforce managers may wish to address. For example, if employees report leaving for private-sector jobs that offer higher pay or greater opportunities for advancement, or leaving for civilian positions in another part of the federal government due to lack of advancement opportunities in the same geographic location, workforce managers may be able to offer incentives for such employees to remain, especially in positions that are hard to fill.

Collect information on motivations for moving to the Army from another federal agency. An exit survey should provide information about why civilians leave the Army. However, understanding why civilians in other parts of DoD, or in the federal government as a whole, move *to* the Army can be equally valuable. The Army may provide better career advancement opportunities in certain occupations or locations; if this is the case, Army workforce managers may wish to build on these advantages in recruiting talent from elsewhere in the federal government or to replicate similar conditions in other areas. A short entry survey, targeted at individuals who join the Army civilian workforce from another federal agency, could shed light on this issue.

Consider whether hiring outreach strategies could be modified to increase diversity in higher pay grades. While our analysis of gender differences across career patterns cannot be interpreted as causal, it does suggest that the higher likelihood that women spend a short time in service, or in lower grades, is linked with occupation, prior military service, temporary or term appointments, education, and other factors. If women are disproportionately hired into occupations that have few prospects for career progression, or that typically rely on temporary or term positions rather than career appointments, then it may be difficult to increase female participation in leadership positions. A focused effort to encourage the hiring of women in occupations that are associated with longer-term service in higher grades may improve diversity in the pipeline for leadership positions. Similar targeting with respect to prior military service or education credentials may also be effective.

Examine whether observed career patterns are similar across different segments of the civilian workforce. Our analysis showed that there is substantial variation in career trajectories across career programs; for example, individuals who enter the Information Technology Management program and the Analysis, Modeling, and Simulation program are more likely to spend longer periods of time in the Army. From the point of view of a career program manager, it can be valuable to understand the specific patterns associated with entrants into those programs, in order to offer more effective career guidance to employees and to build a workforce with the desired mix of experience. Therefore, we recommend a career pattern analysis specific to certain critical segments of the Army civilian workforce, particularly those in which attrition and leader development are expected to be particularly challenging.

Explore whether resources are being effectively applied within the civilian workforce. The cluster analysis highlighted that the majority of entrants into the Army civilian workforce spend a relatively short amount of time there. Since the resources available for training those civilians—in terms of both money and time—are limited, it is important that they be applied efficiently and effectively. A first step toward this goal would be to systematically document how training resources are distributed across geographic locations, commands, and career programs, as well as how they are distributed across individual career stages (for example, new entrants versus midcareer civilians). Further analysis could then examine whether the application of those training resources is associated with desired retention and promotion outcomes.

This research has shown that there is substantial diversity in the career trajectories that Army civilians follow. Many of them join the Army civilian workforce at an early stage in their careers and spend 20 or more years there; among this group, a substantial share progress to midlevel grades, and a smaller share to higher grades. However, a majority of entrants spend only a few years in the Army civilian workforce. Most of these individuals leave the DoD civilian workforce entirely, but a sizable share move to other DoD components, and some return after a gap in service. Systematically gathering information on the reasons behind employee departure and mobility, examining career patterns in more detail in critical segments of the civilian workforce, and documenting how training resources are currently used and whether they are associated with desired outcomes can help Army workforce managers improve workforce management in key locations and career programs, and enhance the pipeline for future Army leadership.

Creating the Dissimilarity Matrix Using Optimal Matching

We know the pay grade of each Army civilian employee in the sample for each year of service. We create career patterns that represent groups of Army civilian employees who have similar patterns of pay grades throughout a career. For this analysis, we created groups of pay grades that are meaningful in terms of career transitions. We used four groupings of pay grades to identify each civilian's status for each year of his or her career: GS 0–9, GS 10–12, GS 13–15, and SES.

To create the dissimilarity matrix, which provides the basic data for the cluster analysis, the OM method applies transformations to each pair of sequences in order to make the sequences identical. Each transformation has a "cost." There are three kinds of transformations: insertion, deletion, and substitution; and OM proceeds by applying the transformations in a way that minimizes the "cost" of making each sequence identical to every other sequence. The final "cost" matrix is the dissimilarity matrix.

To create the dissimilarity matrix, the costs of the substitution, insertion, and deletion transformations need to be set. The substitution cost matrix (Table A.2) is derived from the transition rates observed in the data (Table A.1). Note that transition rates are bidirectional and not symmetrical. Substitution costs are calculated using the two transition rates for each pair of states (e.g., A to B and B to A) and are symmetrical (Table A.2). Generally speaking, less probable transitions between each pair of states result in higher substitution costs. The substitution cost matrix is calculated from the transition rate (TRATE) matrix as follows:

$$substitution\ cost_{i,j} = cval - P_{i,j} - P_{j,i}$$

where:
  $cval$ is the constant substitution cost and is set to 2
  $P_{i,j}$ is the transition rate from state i to j
  $P_{j,i}$ is the transition rate from state j to i.

Insertion and deletion costs are set at a constant cost of 2, the same as the constant substitution cost (*cval*).

Table A.1
Transition Rate Matrix (TRATE)

	Army GS 0–9	Army GS 10–12	Army GS 13–15	Army SES	Other DoD GS 0–9	Other DoD GS 10–12	Other DoD GS 13–15	Other DoD SES	Gap
Army GS 0–9	0.914	0.038	0.000	0.000	0.019	0.001	0.000	0.000	0.028
Army GS 10–12	0.007	0.939	0.033	0.000	0.001	0.010	0.001	0.000	0.009
Army GS 13–15	0.000	0.018	0.969	0.000	0.000	0.001	0.007	0.000	0.005
Army SES	0.000	0.000	0.000	0.980	0.000	0.000	0.000	0.014	0.005
Other DoD GS 0–9	0.057	0.003	0.000	0.000	0.865	0.034	0.000	0.000	0.040
Other DoD GS 10–12	0.003	0.035	0.003	0.000	0.006	0.903	0.031	0.000	0.018
Other DoD GS 13–15	0.000	0.006	0.022	0.000	0.000	0.014	0.947	0.001	0.011
Other DoD SES	0.000	0.000	0.000	0.064	0.000	0.000	0.006	0.931	0.000
Gap	0.156	0.035	0.007	0.000	0.052	0.011	0.003	0.000	0.735

NOTE: Transition rate matrix calculated as part of the hierarchical cluster analysis to identify common career patterns. Authors' calculations based on end-of-year snapshots from the DMDC Civilian Master Files from FY 1980 to FY 2015.

Table A.2
Substitution Cost Matrix

	Army GS 0–9	Army GS 10–12	Army GS 13–15	Army SES	Other DoD GS 0–9	Other DoD GS 10–12	Other DoD GS 13–15	Other DoD SES	Gap
Army GS 0–9	0.00	1.96	2.00	2.00	1.92	2.00	2.00	2.00	1.82
Army GS 10–12	1.96	0.00	1.95	2.00	2.00	1.95	1.99	2.00	1.96
Army GS 13–15	2.00	1.95	0.00	2.00	2.00	2.00	1.97	2.00	1.99
Army SES	2.00	2.00	2.00	0.00	2.00	2.00	2.00	1.92	1.99
Other DoD GS 0–9	1.92	2.00	2.00	2.00	0.00	1.96	2.00	2.00	1.91
Other DoD GS 10–12	2.00	1.95	2.00	2.00	1.96	0.00	1.96	2.00	1.97
Other DoD GS 13–15	2.00	1.99	1.97	2.00	2.00	1.96	0.00	1.99	1.99
Other DoD SES	2.00	2.00	2.00	1.92	2.00	2.00	1.99	0.00	2.00
Gap	1.82	1.96	1.99	1.99	1.91	1.97	1.99	2.00	0.00

NOTE: Substitution cost matrix calculated as part of the hierarchical cluster analysis to identify common career patterns. Authors' calculations based on end-of-year snapshots from the DMDC Civilian Master Files from FY 1980 to FY 2015.

Career Program Mapping

The data we used for the analysis contained some information about civilians' career program assignments, but not all civilians in the sample were identified with a career program, particularly in early years. However, nearly all observations have an associated four-digit OPM occupational code. Therefore, we created a concordance mapping occupational codes to career programs.

We began with a list of the four-digit occupational codes associated with each of the Army's 31 career programs as of March 2015, provided by our sponsor. Working from this list, we created a unique concordance mapping each occupational series to a career program.

In certain cases, the list provided by the sponsor mapped an occupational series to more than one career program; for example, series 0410 (Zoology) is associated with career program 16 (Engineers and Scientists—Nonconstruction) and career program 53 (Medical). Thus, to facilitate the mapping, we combined a few of the career programs into broader groups. For example, we combined career program 16 (Engineers and Scientists—Nonconstruction), career program 18 (Engineers and Scientists—Resources and Construction), and career program 53 (Medical) into the Engineering, Science, and Medical group. In addition, we identified individuals who entered any occupational series as a "trainee" as a separate trainee group.

In some instances, an occupational series that appeared in the dataset did not appear in the list provided by the sponsor. In these cases, we assigned a career program based on information from the dataset on which career programs were most commonly associated with the occupational series (where career program was available), along with OPM's description of the occupational series. In addition, the dataset contained several occupational series that did not appear in the most current version of the *Handbook of Occupational Groups and Families* from OPM (2009). For these series, we assigned a career program based on the career programs associated with similar occupational codes.

Table B.1 shows our mapping of occupational series to career program groups. We list only those occupational series for which an individual in our sample was first observed in that series.

Table B.1
Mapping Occupational Series to Career Programs

Occupational Series	Career Program Group	Included Career Programs
0142, 0160, 0201, 0203, 0204, 0205, 0212, 0221, 0222, 0223, 0230, 0233, 0235, 0246, 0260, 0360, 0361	Human resource management	10 (Civilian Human Resource Management), 28 (Equal Opportunity Employment), 50 (Military Personnel Management)
0343, 0501, 0503, 0504, 0505, 0510, 0511, 0525, 0530, 0540, 0544, 0545, 0560, 0561, 0590, 0592, 1160	Comptroller	11 (Comptroller)
0018, 0019, 0081, 0690, 0803, 1306, 1815, 1825	Safety and occupational health management	12 (Safety and Occupational Health Management)
0050, 0346, 1104, 1107, 1120, 1658, 1667, 2001, 2003, 2005, 2010, 2030, 2032, 2050, 2091	Supply management	13 (Supply Management)
1101, 1102, 1103, 1105, 1106	Contracting and acquisition	14 (Contracting and Acquisition)
1910, 1960	Quality assurance	15 (Quality and Reliability Assurance), 20 (Quality Assurance Specialist—Ammunition Surveillance)
0020, 0021, 0023, 0025, 0026, 0028, 0029, 0062, 0090, 0101, 0102, 0110, 0119, 0150, 0180, 0181, 0184, 0185, 0186, 0190, 0193, 0401, 0403, 0404, 0405,0408, 0410, 0413, 0414, 0415, 0430, 0437, 0454, 0455, 0457, 0458, 0460, 0462, 0470, 0471, 0480, 0482, 0486, 0493, 0601, 0602, 0603, 0610, 0620, 0621, 0622, 0625, 0630, 0631, 0633, 0635, 0636, 0638, 0640, 0642, 0644, 0645, 0646, 0647, 0648, 0649, 0651, 0660, 0661, 0662, 0665, 0667, 0668, 0669, 0670, 0671, 0673, 0675, 0679, 0680, 0681, 0682, 0683, 0684, 0688, 0698, 0701, 0704, 0801, 0802, 0804, 0806, 0807, 0808, 0809, 0810, 0817, 0818, 0819, 0830, 0840, 0850, 0854, 0855, 0858, 0861, 0871, 0880, 0892, 0893, 0894, 0896, 0962, 1008, 1130, 1170, 1171, 1176, 1301, 1310, 1311, 1313, 1315, 1316, 1320, 1321, 1340, 1341, 1350, 1360, 1361, 1370, 1371, 1372, 1373, 1374, 1382, 1384, 1510, 1520, 1521, 1529, 1530, 1531, 1550, 1640	Engineering, science, and medical	16 (Engineering and Scientists—Nonconstruction), 18 (Engineers and Scientists—Resources and Construction), 53 (Medical)
0856, 0873, 0895, 1083, 1152, 1601, 1670	Materiel maintenance management	17 (Materiel Maintenance Management)
0006, 0007, 0072, 0083, 0085, 1397, 1802, 1810, 1811, 1812, 1890, 1897	Security	19 (Physical Security and Law Enforcement)
1035, 1081, 1082, 1087	Public affairs and communications media	22 (Public Affairs and Communications Media)

Table B.1—Continued

Occupational Series	Career Program Group	Included Career Programs
2101, 2102, 2130, 2131, 2132, 2133, 2134, 2135, 2144, 2150, 2151, 2161	Transportation and distribution management	24 (Transportation and Distribution Management)
1173	Housing management	27 (Housing Management)
0030, 0187, 0188, 0189, 1051, 1054, 1056, 1144	Installation management	29 (Installation Management)
0060, 1701, 1702, 1710, 1712, 1720, 1724, 1740, 1750, 1755	Education and training	31 (Education Services), 32 (Training, Capabilities, and Doctrine Warfighting Development)
1150	Ammunition management	33 (Ammunition Management)
0332, 0334, 0335, 0382, 0390, 0391, 0392, 0393, 0394, 1001, 1020, 1021, 1060, 1071, 1084, 1410, 1411, 1412, 1515	IT and modeling	34 (Information Technology Management), 36 (Analysis, Modeling, and Simulation)
0080, 0086, 0132, 0134	Intelligence	35 (Intelligence)
0301, 0302, 0303, 0304, 0305, 0309, 0312, 0313, 0316, 0318, 0319, 0322, 0326, 0330, 0340, 0341, 0342, 0344, 0345, 0350, 0351, 0355, 0356, 0357, 0359, 0385, 0388, 0389, 0904, 0905, 0930, 0950, 0963, 0967, 0986, 0990, 0992, 0998, 1221, 1222, 1654	Administration, management, and legal	51 (General Administration and Management), 56 (Legal)
1801	Inspector General	55 (Inspector General)
0130, 0131, 1040, 1045, 1046	Foreign affairs and strategic planning	60 (Foreign Affairs and Strategic Planning)
0170, 1010, 1015, 1016, 1420, 1421	Historian/museum curator	61 (Historian/Museum Curator)
2152, 2154, 2181, 2183, 2185	Aviation	64 (Aviation)
0099, 0199, 0299, 0399, 0499, 0599, 0699, 0899, 0999, 1099, 1199, 1399, 1499, 1599, 1699, 1799, 1899, 2099, 2199	Trainee	None (Trainee)

NOTE: Only occupational series codes that appear in the data we used in the cluster analysis are shown here.

Summary Statistics for Sample

Table C.1 provides summary statistics of key characteristics for the sample of 180,000 individuals used in the cluster analysis. Note that the distribution of characteristics by entrant does not necessarily represent the overall composition of the Army civilian workforce at any given time. This sample reflects restrictions described in Chapter Two, most notably inclusion of individuals entering between FY 1981 and FY 2000, and who were observed at least twice. In addition, the average characteristics are for entrants, rather than for the population on board at any given point in time. For example, although Table C.1 shows that nearly 60 percent of entrants are women, fewer than 40 percent of individuals in the Army civilian workforce at the end of FY 2015 were female. An important reason for this difference is that women tend to spend shorter amounts of time in the Army civilian workforce, and so they make up a larger share of entrants than they do of the workforce at any given point in time.

Table C.1
Summary Statistics for Sample

	Percentage of Entrants
Gender	
Male	40.9
Female	59.1
Race	
Asian	3.94
Black	18.72
Hispanic	5.15
Other	1.14
White	71.06

Table C.1—Continued

	Percentage of Entrants
Age at entry	
25 or below	24.36
26–32	27.31
33–40	23.98
41 or above	24.35
Education at entry	
College	18.05
High school	38.34
Less than high school	1.47
Other	4.97
Postgraduate	8.40
Some college	28.76
Veteran status	
Nonveteran	63.93
Veteran	29.44
Retired military	6.62
Entered on a temp/term appointment	34.9
Entered in supervisory role	2.60
Entered in D.C. metro area	7.59
Months of federal service at entry	
<1 year	58.2
1–5 years	23.7
5+ years	18.2
Participated in NSPS	12.91

Table C.1—Continued

	Percentage of Entrants
Career program at entry	
Administration, management, and legal	34.6
Ammunition management	0.1
Aviation	0.6
Comptroller	6.7
Contracting and acquisition	2.2
Education and training	4.7
Engineering, science, and medical	21.5
Foreign affairs and strategic planning	0.04
Historian/museum curator	0.1
Housing management	0.1
Human resource management	4.4
Inspector general	0.03
IT and modeling	5.2
Installation management	2.3
Intelligence	0.5
Materiel maintenance management	1.3
Public affairs and communications media	0.5
Quality assurance	0.4
Safety and occupational health management	1.6
Security	2.0
Supply management	7.0
Trainee	2.8
Transportation and distribution management	1.3

NOTE: Authors' calculations based on DMDC Civilian Master Files from FY 1980 to FY 2015. Only individuals included in the statistical cluster analysis are included.

Regression Results

This appendix presents the full set of results associated with the multinomial logistic regressions presented in Chapter Four, as well as results for the relationship between career pattern membership and additional characteristics.

Table D.1 presents the marginal effects from a multinomial logistic regression of the probability of being in each career pattern given individual and job characteristics. Career pattern descriptions are shown in column headings. Effects are shown relative to omitted categories: omitted race is white; omitted category of age at entry is 25 or below; omitted educational category at entry is college; omitted cohort is 1981–1985; omitted years of federal service at entry is less than one; and omitted career program group is Administration, Management, and Legal.

Chapter Four presented the results on career pattern membership, and on the relationship between career pattern and characteristics as shown in Table D.1, for gender, prior military service, and career program. The remainder of this appendix contains similar results for other characteristics.

Race and Ethnicity

Figures D.1a, D.1b, and D.1c explore the relationship between career pattern and race and ethnicity. Figure D.1a shows that the overall continuation pattern is similar across race and ethnicity, but continuation probabilities between 5 and 20 YOS are slightly lower for black than for white and Hispanic individuals. Meanwhile, continuation probabilities are slightly higher for Asians across most YOS.[1]

---

[1] A log-rank test finds that the curves are statistically different across race and ethnicity ($p < .0001$).

Table D.1
Relationship Between Career Pattern and Individual and Job Characteristics

	Short-Term	Mid-Grade	Low-Grade	High-Grade	Multiple Components, Low-Grade	Multiple Components, Higher Grades	Long Gap
Female	0.0248***	−0.0504***	0.0226***	−0.0350***	0.0262***	−0.00172	0.0134***
	(0.00282)	(0.00182)	(0.00182)	(0.00104)	(0.00118)	(0.00113)	(0.00102)
Asian	−0.0872***	0.00547	0.0199***	−0.00460*	0.0413***	0.0193***	0.00587*
	(0.00588)	(0.00366)	(0.00391)	(0.00202)	(0.00324)	(0.00277)	(0.00241)
Black	−0.00249	−0.0170***	0.0204***	−0.0102***	0.0128***	−0.00168	−0.00183
	(0.00293)	(0.00194)	(0.00182)	(0.00127)	(0.00121)	(0.00117)	(0.00103)
Hispanic	−0.0214***	−0.00927**	0.0193***	−0.0101***	0.0244***	−0.00377	0.000773
	(0.00505)	(0.00321)	(0.00319)	(0.00195)	(0.00242)	(0.00200)	(0.00189)
Other	−0.0182	−0.00634	0.0122	−0.00474	0.00659	0.00746	0.00304
	(0.0105)	(0.00673)	(0.00648)	(0.00453)	(0.00412)	(0.00487)	(0.00431)
Age 26–32	−0.0431***	0.0137***	0.0373***	−0.00788***	0.0142***	−0.000627	−0.0135***
	(0.00325)	(0.00209)	(0.00186)	(0.00163)	(0.00119)	(0.00150)	(0.00176)
Age 33–40	−0.0700***	0.0384***	0.0614***	−0.0119***	0.0211***	−0.00538***	−0.0335***
	(0.00346)	(0.00230)	(0.00207)	(0.00174)	(0.00133)	(0.00156)	(0.00173)
Age 41 or above	0.115***	0.0159***	−0.0101***	−0.0345***	0.000738	−0.0294***	−0.0580***
	(0.00336)	(0.00224)	(0.00180)	(0.00160)	(0.00125)	(0.00139)	(0.00159)
High school	0.0798***	−0.0869***	0.0755***	−0.0529***	0.0251***	−0.0336***	−0.00706***
	(0.00340)	(0.00237)	(0.00185)	(0.00151)	(0.00120)	(0.00156)	(0.00135)
Less than high school	0.126***	−0.117***	0.0701***	−0.0627***	0.0255***	−0.0342***	−0.00780*
	(0.00960)	(0.00579)	(0.00672)	(0.00276)	(0.00406)	(0.00367)	(0.00343)
Other	0.0378***	−0.0911***	0.0876***	−0.0552***	0.0433***	−0.0237***	0.00134
	(0.00578)	(0.00371)	(0.00360)	(0.00218)	(0.00256)	(0.00251)	(0.00237)
Postgraduate	0.00506	−0.0118***	−0.0239***	0.0323***	−0.00945***	0.00577*	0.00201
	(0.00471)	(0.00325)	(0.00178)	(0.00260)	(0.00138)	(0.00251)	(0.00219)
Some college	0.0658***	−0.0622***	0.0571***	−0.0509***	0.0211***	−0.0287***	−0.00226
	(0.00349)	(0.00248)	(0.00183)	(0.00154)	(0.00125)	(0.00160)	(0.00141)
Nonretired veteran	−0.0358***	0.00294	0.00347	−0.00474***	0.00412**	0.00611***	0.0239***
	(0.00312)	(0.00193)	(0.00189)	(0.00119)	(0.00135)	(0.00128)	(0.00142)

Table D.1—Continued

	Short-Term	Mid-Grade	Low-Grade	High-Grade	Multiple Components, Low-Grade	Multiple Components, Higher Grades	Long Gap
Retired veteran	−0.296***	0.0355***	0.0367***	0.0296***	0.00792**	0.0251***	0.161***
	(0.00576)	(0.00340)	(0.00435)	(0.00272)	(0.00288)	(0.00310)	(0.00723)
1–5 yrs federal service	0.00875**	0.000853	0.00577**	−0.00750***	−0.00290*	−0.00478***	−0.000186
	(0.00289)	(0.00189)	(0.00179)	(0.00117)	(0.00120)	(0.00116)	(0.00110)
5+ yrs federal service	0.0110**	0.00598**	−0.00562**	0.000951	−0.00943***	−0.00446**	0.00155
	(0.00337)	(0.00217)	(0.00200)	(0.00147)	(0.00128)	(0.00136)	(0.00141)
Supervisor	0.0107	0.0342***	−0.0504***	0.00763**	−0.00905**	0.0107***	−0.00388
	(0.00695)	(0.00439)	(0.00370)	(0.00256)	(0.00325)	(0.00310)	(0.00280)
Entered in D.C.	0.0238***	−0.0187***	−0.0354***	0.0167***	−0.00289	0.0186***	−0.00215
	(0.00409)	(0.00261)	(0.00213)	(0.00196)	(0.00168)	(0.00198)	(0.00158)
Career appointment	−0.105***	0.0411***	0.0303***	0.0222***	0.00692***	0.0105***	−0.00636***
	(0.00242)	(0.00156)	(0.00143)	(0.000948)	(0.000967)	(0.000983)	(0.000957)
1986–90 cohort	0.0150***	−0.0126***	−0.00157	0.00163	−0.000874	−0.00605***	0.00446***
	(0.00262)	(0.00165)	(0.00171)	(0.00102)	(0.00111)	(0.00107)	(0.00101)
1991–95 cohort	0.00700*	0.00474*	−0.0151***	0.0102***	−0.00904***	−0.00857***	0.0108***
	(0.00337)	(0.00217)	(0.00214)	(0.00138)	(0.00139)	(0.00135)	(0.00137)
1996–2000 cohort	0.0677***	0.0415***	−0.0866***	0.0193***	−0.0203***	−0.0142***	−0.00740***
	(0.00363)	(0.00274)	(0.00151)	(0.00173)	(0.00134)	(0.00144)	(0.00125)
Ammunition management	−0.169***	0.160***	−0.0887***	0.0485**	−0.0423***	0.0863***	0.00491
	(0.0402)	(0.0313)	(0.0143)	(0.0185)	(0.000753)	(0.0262)	(0.0207)
Aviation	−0.0469***	0.0326***	−0.103***	0.155***	−0.0355***	0.00371	−0.00602
	(0.0137)	(0.00848)	(0.00328)	(0.00941)	(0.00399)	(0.00640)	(0.00560)
Comptroller	−0.0582***	0.0307***	−0.0420***	0.00916***	0.0222***	0.0368***	0.00127
	(0.00477)	(0.00315)	(0.00255)	(0.00200)	(0.00234)	(0.00245)	(0.00182)
Contracting and acquisition	−0.0425***	0.0322***	−0.0477***	0.0104***	−0.0133***	0.0486***	0.0122***
	(0.00772)	(0.00484)	(0.00420)	(0.00288)	(0.00304)	(0.00420)	(0.00363)
Education and training	0.0168**	0.0316***	−0.0115**	−0.0108***	−0.0104***	−0.0148***	−0.000890
	(0.00556)	(0.00357)	(0.00372)	(0.00187)	(0.00226)	(0.00180)	(0.00214)

Table D.1—Continued

	Short-Term	Mid-Grade	Low-Grade	High-Grade	Multiple Components, Low-Grade	Multiple Components, Higher Grades	Long Gap
Engineering, science, and medical	0.00205	0.0332***	−0.0170***	0.0122***	−0.0277***	−0.00737***	0.00447***
	(0.00332)	(0.00218)	(0.00215)	(0.00138)	(0.00105)	(0.00121)	(0.00131)
Foreign affairs and strategic planning	0.0142	0.0407	−0.0511	0.0251	−0.0423***	0.0151	−0.00173
	(0.0519)	(0.0343)	(0.0318)	(0.0215)	(0.000753)	(0.0243)	(0.0212)
Historian/ museum curator	−0.132***	0.0807***	0.0367	0.0212*	0.00340	0.00112	−0.0108
	(0.0360)	(0.0207)	(0.0334)	(0.00951)	(0.0218)	(0.0104)	(0.0107)
Housing management	−0.0709	0.0298	−0.0238	0.00883	0.00378	0.0448*	0.00753
	(0.0381)	(0.0223)	(0.0240)	(0.0152)	(0.0181)	(0.0218)	(0.0172)
Human resource management	0.0173**	−0.00139	−0.00819*	−0.0112***	−0.0133***	0.0116***	0.00522*
	(0.00554)	(0.00347)	(0.00345)	(0.00207)	(0.00199)	(0.00257)	(0.00217)
Inspector General	−0.0166	0.104*	−0.0544	0.0362	−0.0423***	−0.0155	−0.0112
	(0.0598)	(0.0427)	(0.0366)	(0.0251)	(0.000753)	(0.0191)	(0.0209)
Installation management	0.0898***	−0.0454***	−0.0127**	−0.0208***	−0.0115***	0.000936	−0.000295
	(0.00716)	(0.00369)	(0.00485)	(0.00227)	(0.00288)	(0.00315)	(0.00273)
Intelligence	0.156***	−0.0182*	−0.0855***	−0.0188***	−0.0285***	0.000664	−0.00552
	(0.0127)	(0.00714)	(0.00596)	(0.00310)	(0.00520)	(0.00564)	(0.00548)
IT and modeling	−0.0416***	0.0572***	−0.0365***	0.0150***	−0.0142***	0.0252***	−0.00510**
	(0.00530)	(0.00367)	(0.00309)	(0.00220)	(0.00204)	(0.00254)	(0.00188)
Materiel maintenance management	−0.0881***	0.156***	−0.0727***	0.0340***	−0.0294***	0.00835	−0.00791*
	(0.0102)	(0.00813)	(0.00438)	(0.00496)	(0.00319)	(0.00465)	(0.00394)
Public affairs and communications media	0.00137	0.0449***	−0.0359***	0.000260	−0.0253***	0.0125	0.00224
	(0.0155)	(0.0100)	(0.0102)	(0.00499)	(0.00533)	(0.00649)	(0.00623)
Quality assurance	−0.149***	0.130***	−0.0796***	0.0168**	−0.0295***	0.0956***	0.0151
	(0.0183)	(0.0132)	(0.00712)	(0.00630)	(0.00568)	(0.0118)	(0.00898)
Safety and occupational health management	−0.192***	−0.0180***	0.112***	−0.00728**	0.120***	−0.00278	−0.0122***
	(0.00964)	(0.00442)	(0.00808)	(0.00273)	(0.00855)	(0.00329)	(0.00263)
Security	0.0874***	−0.0584***	0.0110*	−0.0178***	0.00897*	−0.0228***	−0.00829**
	(0.00773)	(0.00306)	(0.00543)	(0.00252)	(0.00429)	(0.00221)	(0.00284)

Table D.1—Continued

	Short-Term	Mid-Grade	Low-Grade	High-Grade	Multiple Components, Low-Grade	Multiple Components, Higher Grades	Long Gap
Supply management	−0.0107*	0.00690*	−0.0261***	0.00190	0.0229***	−0.000504	0.00572**
	(0.00465)	(0.00309)	(0.00252)	(0.00217)	(0.00214)	(0.00192)	(0.00182)
Trainee	0.0741***	0.0190***	−0.0584***	0.0106***	−0.0306***	−0.0104***	−0.00432
	(0.00666)	(0.00484)	(0.00355)	(0.00300)	(0.00188)	(0.00233)	(0.00241)
Transportation and distribution management	−0.0237*	0.00913	−0.0282***	0.0221***	0.0161**	0.0135**	−0.00884**
	(0.00999)	(0.00612)	(0.00553)	(0.00493)	(0.00492)	(0.00473)	(0.00322)
Observations	180,000	180,000	180,000	180,000	180,000	180,000	180,000

NOTE: Marginal effects based on a multinomial logistic regression of the probability of being in each career pattern on the observable characteristics listed in the table. Standard errors in parentheses. Column headings show career pattern names. Effects are relative to omitted categories. Omitted race is white; omitted category of age at entry is 25 or below; omitted educational category at entry is college; omitted cohort is 1981–85; and omitted career program group is Administration, Management, and Legal. *, **, and *** represent statistical significance at the 10, 5, and 1 percent levels, respectively.

Figure D.1a
Continuation Curves by Race and Ethnicity

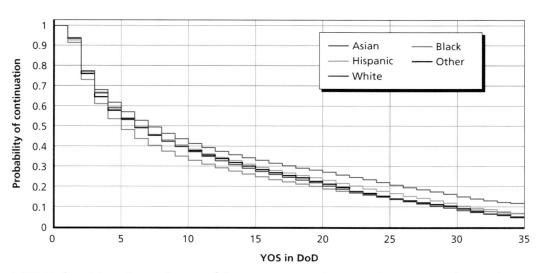

NOTE: Kaplan-Meier estimates, by race, of the continuation probabilities after each year of service for employees in the hierarchical cluster analysis. Individuals are identified as departing the first time they are no longer observed in an end-of-FY snapshot, and are observed until the end of FY 2015 or until they leave the DoD civilian workforce. Authors' calculations based on end-of-year snapshots from the DMDC Civilian Master Files from FY 1980 to FY 2015.

RAND *RR2280A-D.1a*

Figure D.1b
Distribution of Career Patterns by Race and Ethnicity

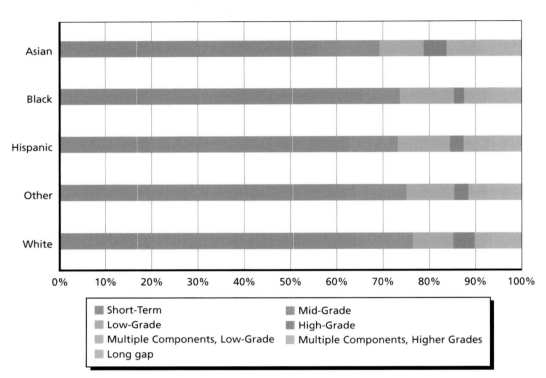

NOTE: Percentage of individual career trajectories identified with each career pattern, by race. Authors' calculations based on hierarchical clustering analysis using end-of-year snapshots from the DMDC Civilian Master Files from FY 1980 to FY 2015.
RAND RR2280A-D.1b

Figures D.1b and D.1c show that the distribution of individuals across career patterns differs somewhat by race and ethnicity, although the differences are not as stark as the differences by gender. In Figure D.1c, the magnitude of the bars can be interpreted as the percentage point difference in probability of career pattern membership for individuals identified as black, Hispanic, Asian, or other, relative to those identified as white.

After controlling for other observable characteristics, black and Hispanic individuals are more likely to be in one of the low-grade career patterns (Low-Grade; Multiple Components, Low-Grade) and less likely to be in the Mid-Grade or High-Grade patterns. Hispanics are also less likely to be in the Short-Term pattern.

Asians are also more likely to be in one of the low-grade patterns and less likely to be in the Short-Term pattern. However, they are also more likely to spend time in other DoD services at higher grades (Multiple Components, Higher Grades).

Figure D.1c
Marginal Effects of Race and Ethnicity on Career Pattern (Relative to Individuals Identified as White)

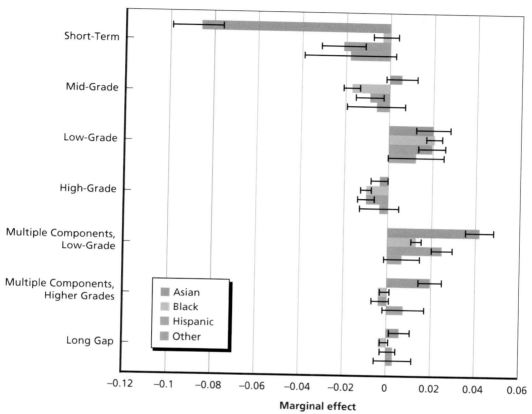

NOTE: Marginal effect of race on probability of being in each career pattern. Results are based on a multinomial logistic regression of the probability of being in each career pattern, and can be interpreted as the percentage point difference in probability of career pattern membership, relative to individuals identified as white. Black bars indicate 95 percent confidence intervals. Authors' calculations based on hierarchical clustering and regression analysis using end-of-year snapshots from the DMDC Civilian Master Files from FY 1980 to FY 2015.

RAND RR2280A-D.1c

Age at Entry

Figure D.2a shows continuation curves by age of entry into the DoD civilian work-force.[2] In early YOS, older ages at entry are associated with higher continuation probabilities. After five YOS, the probability of continuation among those who entered at

---

[2] A log-rank test finds that the curves are statistically different across age groups ($p < .0001$).

Figure D.2a
Continuation Curves by Age at Entry

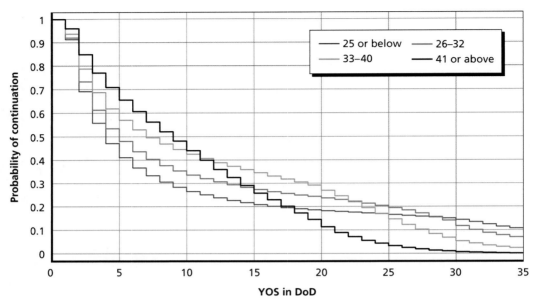

NOTE: Kaplan-Meier estimates, by age at entry into the DoD civilian workforce, of the continuation probabilities after each year of service for employees in the hierarchical cluster analysis. Individuals are identified as departing the first time they are no longer observed in an end-of-FY snapshot, and are observed until the end of FY 2015 or until they leave the DoD civilian workforce. Authors' calculations based on end-of-year snapshots from the DMDC Civilian Master Files from FY 1980 to FY 2015.

RAND *RR2280A-D.2a*

the ages of 41 or above is about 65 percent, compared with 40 percent among those who entered at the ages of 25 or below.

However, this pattern reverses in later YOS, when the continuation curves for those entering at a younger age drop off less quickly. By 20 YOS, the continuation probability is lowest among those who entered at 41 or older, as these workers are likely to become eligible for retirement.

Figures D.2b and D.2c show how the distribution of individuals across career patterns differs by age at entry. In Figure D.2c, the magnitude of the bars can be interpreted as the percentage point difference in probability of career pattern membership for individuals for the specified age at entry, relative to those who enter at the age of 25 or below.

Membership patterns for those entering between the ages of 26 and 32 and between the ages of 33 and 40 are similar. These individuals are less likely to exhibit short-term service than those who enter below the age of 25. They are also more likely to be identified with low-grade and mid-grade patterns (Low-Grade; Mid-Grade; and

Figure D.2b
Distribution of Career Patterns by Age at Entry

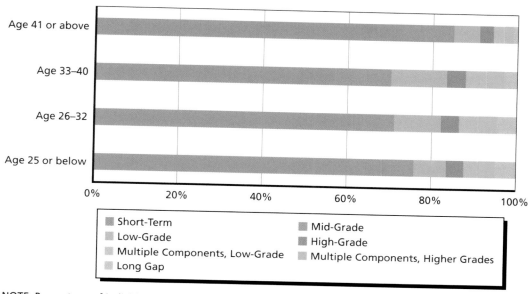

NOTE: Percentage of individual career trajectories identified with each career pattern, by age when initially observed in DoD civilian workforce. Authors' calculations based on hierarchical clustering analysis using end-of-year snapshots from the DMDC Civilian Master Files from FY 1980 to FY 2015.
RAND RR2280A-D.2b

Multiple Components, Low-Grade), and less likely to be identified with higher-grade patterns (High-Grade; Multiple Components, Higher Grades).[3] Both of these groups are also less likely to exhibit a gap in service.

Like those entering between the ages of 26 and 40, those entering at age 41 or above are more likely than those entering at age 25 or below to be in the Mid-Grade pattern, less likely to be in a higher-grade pattern, and less likely to exhibit a gap in service. However, they are 12 percentage points *more* likely than those entering at age 25 or below to be in the Short-Term career pattern.

Overall, the results for age at entry suggest that the youngest and oldest entrants into the DoD civilian workforce are those most likely to serve for a short amount of time. However, young entrants are the most likely to eventually be promoted to the highest GS levels in the Army or in other parts of DoD.

---

[3] The coefficient on Multiple Components, Higher Grades is not statistically significant at the 5 percent level for the 26–32 age group.

Figure D.2c
Marginal Effects of Age at Entry on Career Pattern (Relative to Those Age 25 or Below)

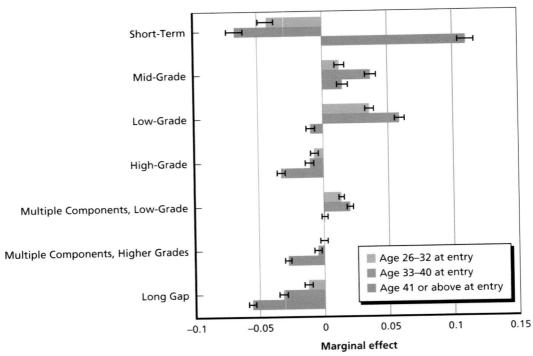

NOTE: Marginal effect of age at entry on probability of being in each career pattern. Results are based on a multinomial logistic regression of the probability of being in each career pattern, and can be interpreted as the percentage point difference in probability of career pattern membership, relative to individuals who were first observed in the DoD civilian workforce at the age of 25 or below. Black bars indicate 95 percent confidence intervals. Authors' calculations based on hierarchical clustering and regression analysis using end-of-year snapshots from the DMDC Civilian Master Files from FY 1980 to FY 2015.

RAND *RR2280A-D.2c*

Education at Entry

Figure D.3a shows that continuation probabilities at any YOS are generally increasing with education level at entry.[4] After five YOS, the probability of continuation among entrants with a college or postgraduate degree is about 60 percent, compared with about 50 percent among entrants with a high school diploma, and 35 percent among those with less than a high school diploma. The gap in survival rates narrows by 20 YOS, but the same pattern remains.

Figures D.3b and D.3c show the distribution of individuals across career patterns by education at entry. In Figure D.3c, the magnitude of the bars can be interpreted as the percentage point difference in probability of career pattern membership for indi-

---

4   A log-rank test finds that the curves are statistically different across education groups ($p < .0001$).

Figure D.3a
Continuation Curves by Education at Entry

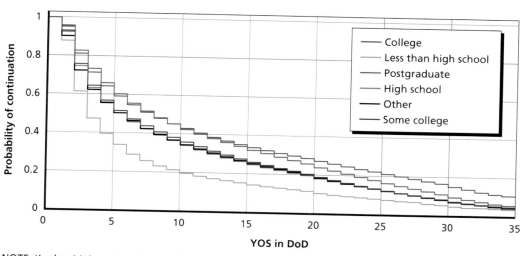

NOTE: Kaplan-Meier estimates, by education at entry into the DoD civilian workforce, of the continuation probabilities after each year of service for employees in the hierarchical cluster analysis. Individuals are identified as departing the first time they are no longer observed in an end-of-FY snapshot, and are observed until the end of FY 2015 or until they leave the DoD civilian workforce. Authors' calculations based on end-of-year snapshots from the DMDC Civilian Master Files from FY 1980 to FY 2015.

RAND RR2280A-D.3a

Figure D.3b
Distribution of Career Patterns by Education at Entry

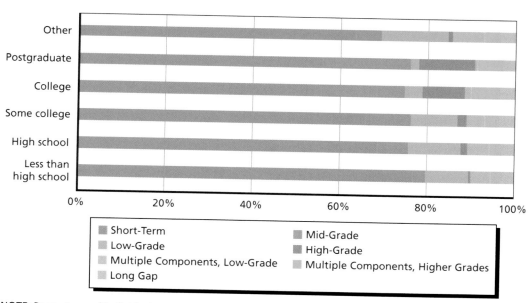

NOTE: Percentage of individual career trajectories identified with each career pattern, by education when initially observed in DoD civilian workforce. Authors' calculations based on hierarchical clustering analysis using end-of-year snapshots from the DMDC Civilian Master Files from FY 1980 to FY 2015.

RAND RR2280A-D.3b

Figure D.3c
Marginal Effects of Education at Entry on Career Pattern (Relative to Those with a College Degree)

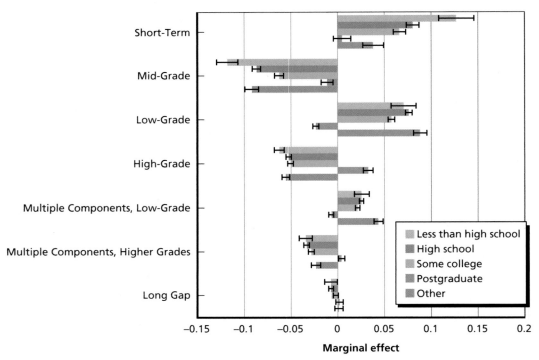

NOTE: Marginal effect of education at entry on probability of being in each career pattern. Results are based on a multinomial logistic regression of the probability of being in each career pattern, and can be interpreted as the percentage point difference in probability of career pattern membership, relative to individuals with a college degree. Black bars indicate 95 percent confidence intervals. Authors' calculations based on hierarchical clustering and regression analysis using end-of-year snapshots from the DMDC Civilian Master Files from FY 1980 to FY 2015.

RAND RR2280A-D.3c

viduals with the specified education at entry, relative to those who entered with a college degree.

Those who entered with less than a college degree are more likely to be in the Short-Term career pattern. The magnitude of the effect (over 12 percentage points) is largest for those without a high school degree. Individuals without a college degree are also more likely to be in the low-grade patterns (Low-Grade; Multiple Components, Low-Grade), and less likely to be in the mid-grade and higher-grade patterns (Mid-Grade; High-Grade; and Multiple Components, Higher Grades).

Those entering with a postgraduate degree are also less likely to be in the Mid-Grade pattern. However, they are less likely to be in the low-grade patterns (Low-Grade; Multiple Components, Low-Grade) and more likely to be in the high-grade patterns (High-Grade; Multiple Components, Higher Grades).

In general, it appears that the relationship between education at entry and career pattern is driven by grade progression, with individuals who have higher education being more likely to progress to higher grades, and therefore to be associated with higher-grade career patterns.

Entry Cohort

Figure D.4a shows continuation curves for the sample, by entry cohort.[5] Similar to the overall patterns noted in Chapter Three, the cohorts entering between FY 1991 and FY 1995 had slightly lower continuation probabilities than the cohorts entering between FY 1981 and FY 1985, likely due to the downsizing that occurred starting in the 1990s. The cohorts entering between FY 1996 and FY 2000 had slightly higher continuation probabilities after 10 YOS; however, as discussed in Chapter Three, the curves for these cohorts terminate by 20 YOS since we observe individuals in these cohorts for a shorter period of time.

Figure D.4a
Continuation Curves by Entry Cohort

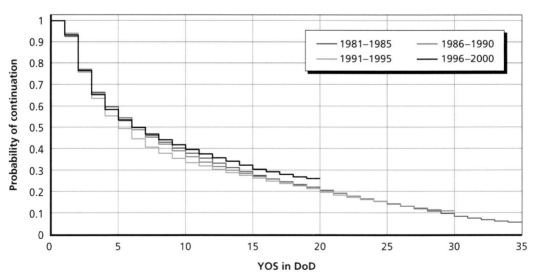

NOTE: Kaplan-Meier estimates, by entry cohort, of the continuation probabilities after each year of service for employees in the hierarchical cluster analysis. Individuals are identified as departing the first time they are no longer observed in an end-of-FY snapshot, and are observed until the end of FY 2015 or until they leave the DoD civilian workforce. Authors' calculations based on end-of-year snapshots from the DMDC Civilian Master Files from FY 1980 to FY 2015.
RAND RR2280A-D.4a

---

[5]   A log-rank test finds that the curves are statistically different across entry cohorts ($p < .0001$).

Figures D.4b and D.4c show the distribution of individuals across career patterns by entry cohort. In Figure D.4c, the magnitude of the bars can be interpreted as the percentage point difference in probability of career pattern membership for individuals in the specified entry cohort, relative to those who entered in FY 1981–1985.

Those who entered in the FY 1986–1990 cohort are more likely to be in the Short-Term career pattern and to exhibit a long gap in service. They are also less likely to be in the Mid-Grade pattern or to serve in other parts of DoD at higher grades (Multiple Components, Higher Grades).

The FY 1991–1995 cohort is less likely to be in the Low-Grade pattern or to spend time in other parts of DoD at any grade (Multiple Components, Low-Grade; Multiple Components, Higher Grades). However, individuals in this cohort are more likely to be in the Mid-Grade and High-Grade career patterns. They are also more likely to be in the Short-Term pattern.

Individuals in the FY 1996–2000 cohort are nearly 7 percentage points more likely than those in the FY 1981–1985 cohort to be in the Short-Term career pattern. They are nearly 9 percentage points less likely to be in the Low-Grade pattern, but are more likely to be in the Mid-Grade and High-Grade patterns. Like the FY 1991–1995 cohort, they are less likely to spend time in other parts of DoD. They are also slightly less likely to exhibit a long gap, although this may be because we cannot observe this

Figure D.4b
Distribution of Career Patterns by Entry Cohort

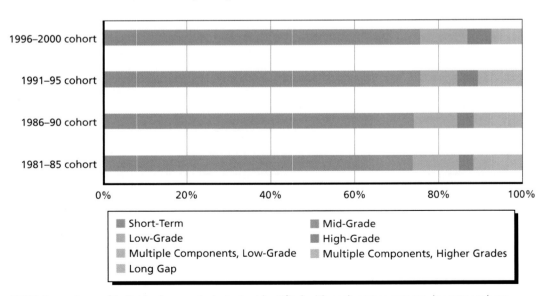

NOTE: Percentage of individual career trajectories identified with each career pattern, by entry cohort. Authors' calculations based on hierarchical clustering analysis using end-of-year snapshots from the DMDC Civilian Master Files from FY 1980 to FY 2015.
RAND RR2280A-D.4b

Figure D.4c
Marginal Effects of Entry Cohort on Career Pattern (Relative to Individuals in the FY 1981–1985 Entry Cohort)

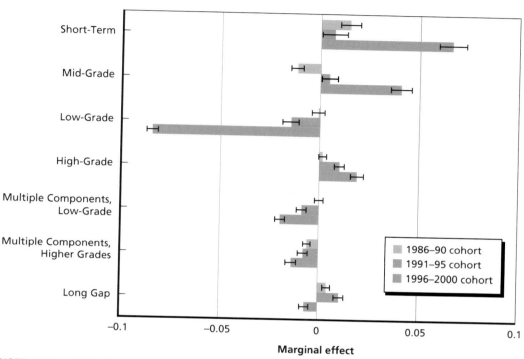

NOTE: Marginal effect of entry cohort on probability of being in each career pattern. Results are based on a multinomial logistic regression of the probability of being in each career pattern, and can be interpreted as the percentage point difference in probability of career pattern membership, relative to individuals in the FY 1981–1985 entry cohort. Black bars indicate 95 percent confidence intervals. Authors' calculations based on hierarchical clustering and regression analysis using end-of-year snapshots from the DMDC Civilian Master Files from FY 1980 to FY 2015.

RAND *RR2280A-D.4c*

cohort for more than 15 to 20 years (and hence we might not observe a reentry that has yet to occur).

While the various entry cohorts exhibit a variety of differing effects, the two most recent cohorts (FY 1991–1995 and FY 1996–2000) are more likely to be in higher-grade patterns and less likely to be in low-grade patterns. This is consistent with the observed increase in GS pay grades of Army civilians over the past 20 years.

Type of Appointment

Figure D.5a shows that the continuation probabilities for those appointed on a temporary or term appointment are much lower than for those appointed on a career

Figure D.5a
Continuation Curves by Appointment Type

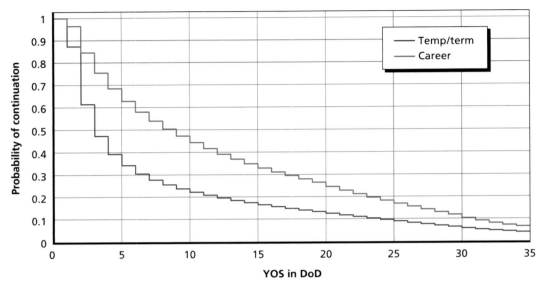

NOTE: Kaplan-Meier estimates, by type of initial appointment, of the continuation probabilities after each year of service for employees in the hierarchical cluster analysis. Individuals are identified as departing the first time they are no longer observed in an end-of-FY snapshot, and are observed until the end of FY 2015 or until they leave the DoD civilian workforce. Authors' calculations based on end-of-year snapshots from the DMDC Civilian Master Files from FY 1980 to FY 2015.
RAND *RR2280A-D.5a*

(or career conditional) appointment.[6] The probability of continuation after five years is approximately 65 percent among those with career appointments, compared with 35 percent among those with temporary or term appointments. Interestingly, among those initially hired with temporary or term appointments, the probability of continuation is about 25 percent after 10 YOS, suggesting that many of these appointments are either renewed or converted to career appointments.

Figures D.5b and D.5c show the distribution of individuals across career patterns by type of appointment. In Figure D.5c, the magnitude of the bars can be interpreted as the percentage point difference in probability of career pattern membership for those initially observed with a career or career conditional appointment, relative to those initially observed with a temporary or term appointment.

As we would expect, those with a career appointment are over 10 percentage points less likely to be in the Short-Term career pattern. They are also slightly less likely to exhibit a gap in service, but are more likely to be in every other career pattern. This

---

[6] A log-rank test finds that the curves are statistically different for temporary versus career appointments ($p < .0001$).

Figure D.5b
Distribution of Career Patterns by Appointment Type

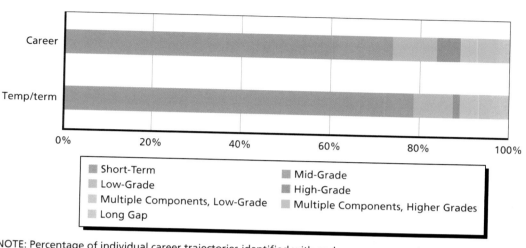

NOTE: Percentage of individual career trajectories identified with each career pattern, by initial type of appointment. Authors' calculations based on hierarchical clustering analysis using end-of-year snapshots from the DMDC Civilian Master Files from FY 1980 to FY 2015.
RAND RR2280A-D.5b

Figure D.5c
Marginal Effects of Career Appointment on Career Pattern (Relative to Those Initially in a Temporary or Term Appointment)

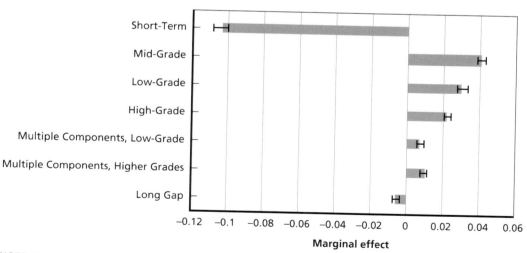

NOTE: Marginal effect of a career or career conditional appointment on probability of being in each career pattern. Results are based on a multinomial logistic regression of the probability of being in each career pattern, and can be interpreted as the percentage point difference in probability of career pattern membership, relative to individuals who were initially hired on a temp or term appointment. Black bars indicate 95 percent confidence intervals. Authors' calculations based on hierarchical clustering and regression analysis using end-of-year snapshots from the DMDC Civilian Master Files from FY 1980 to FY 2015.
RAND RR2280A-D.5c

is consistent with the fact that other than the Short-Term and Long Gap patterns, all of the other career patterns are characterized by relatively long service in the DoD civilian workforce.

Supervisory Status

Figure D.6a shows the continuation curves for those who were first observed in a role with supervisory status, versus those who were not. The probability of continuation is somewhat higher for those first observed in a supervisory role, for the first 15 to 20 YOS. However, the continuation curves are only marginally significantly different ($p = .0946$).

Figures D.6b and D.6c show the distribution of individuals across career patterns by supervisory status at entry. In Figure D.6c, the magnitude of the bars can be interpreted as the percentage point difference in probability of career pattern membership for those initially observed with supervisory status, relative to those initially observed without supervisory status. Those who entered in a supervisory role are less likely to be in a low-grade career pattern and more likely to be in mid-grade and high-grade patterns, both in the Army and in other services.

Figure D.6a
Continuation Curves by Supervisory Status at Entry

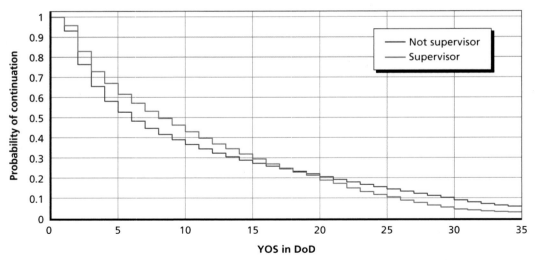

NOTE: Kaplan-Meier estimates, by supervisory status at entry, of the continuation probabilities after each year of service for employees in the hierarchical cluster analysis. Individuals are identified as departing the first time they are no longer observed in an end-of-FY snapshot, and are observed until the end of FY 2015 or until they leave the DoD civilian workforce. Authors' calculations based on end-of-year snapshots from the DMDC Civilian Master Files from FY 1980 to FY 2015.
RAND RR2280A-D.6a

Figure D.6b
Distribution of Career Patterns by Supervisory Status at Entry

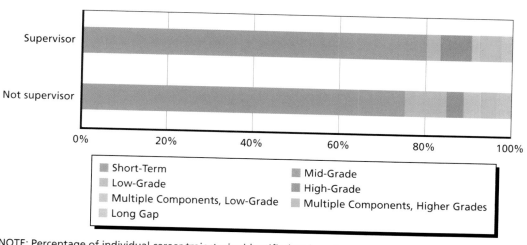

NOTE: Percentage of individual career trajectories identified with each career pattern, by supervisory status at entry. Authors' calculations based on hierarchical clustering analysis using end-of-year snapshots from the DMDC Civilian Master Files from FY 1980 to FY 2015.
RAND *RR2280A-D.6b*

Figure D.6c
Marginal Effects of Supervisory Status at Entry on Career Pattern (Relative to Those Without Supervisory Status at Entry)

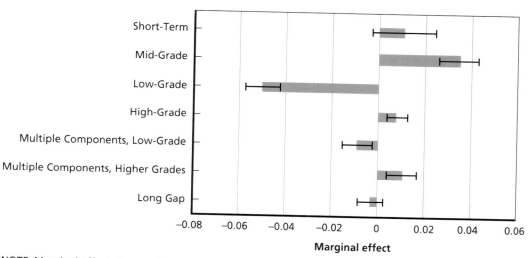

NOTE: Marginal effect of supervisory status at entry on probability of being in each career pattern. Results are based on a multinomial logistic regression of the probability of being in each career pattern, and can be interpreted as the percentage point difference in probability of career pattern membership, relative to individuals who did not have supervisory status at entry. Black bars indicate 95 percent confidence intervals. Authors' calculations based on hierarchical clustering and regression analysis using end-of-year snapshots from the DMDC Civilian Master Files from FY 1980 to FY 2015.
RAND *RR2280A-D.6c*

Years of Federal Service at Entry

Figure D.7a shows the continuation curves for those with no prior federal service when they were first observed, versus those with one to five years, and five or more years.[7] Over the first 20 YOS in the DoD civilian workforce, those with prior federal service generally have higher probabilities of continuation. Interestingly, the major differences do not manifest in the first one or two years of service, during which we might have expected those with no prior federal service to leave in greater numbers, as some of these individuals find that the job is not a good fit. However, we may fail to pick up this effect because we limit the sample to those who are observed at least twice, whereas the expected self-selection effect may occur within the first few months of service.

Consistent with the continuation curves, Figure D.7b shows that those with no prior federal service are more likely to be observed in the Short-Term career pattern. However, after controlling for other observable characteristics, Figure D.7c shows that those with prior federal service are actually more likely to be in the Short-Term career pattern, which suggests that a number of observable characteristics (including, by construction, veteran status) are correlated with prior federal service.

Figure D.7a
Continuation Curves by Years of Federal Service at Entry

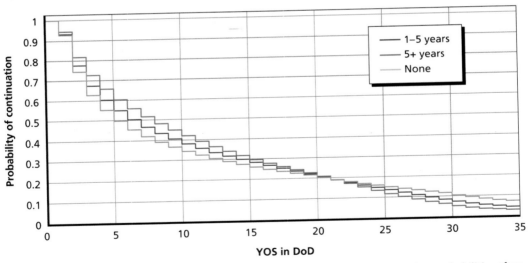

NOTE: Kaplan-Meier estimates, by years of federal service at entry, of the continuation probabilities after each year of service for employees in the hierarchical cluster analysis. Individuals are identified as departing the first time they are no longer observed in an end-of-FY snapshot, and are observed until the end of FY 2015 or until they leave the DoD civilian workforce. Authors' calculations based on end-of-year snapshots from the DMDC Civilian Master Files from FY 1980 to FY 2015.

RAND RR2280A-D.7a

---

7   A log-rank test finds that the curves by years of federal service at entry are statistically different ($p < .0001$).

Figure D.7b
Distribution of Career Patterns by Years of Federal Service at Entry

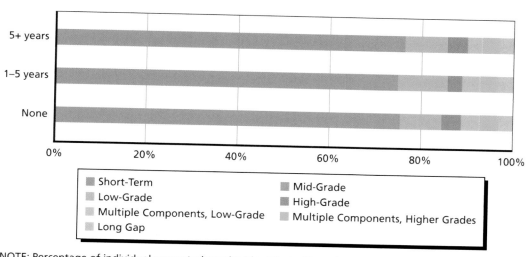

NOTE: Percentage of individual career trajectories identified with each career pattern, by years of federal service at entry. Authors' calculations based on hierarchical clustering analysis using end-of-year snapshots from the DMDC Civilian Master Files from FY 1980 to FY 2015.
RAND *RR2280A-D.7b*

Figure D.7c
Marginal Effects of Years of Federal Service at Entry (Relative to Those with No Federal Service at Entry)

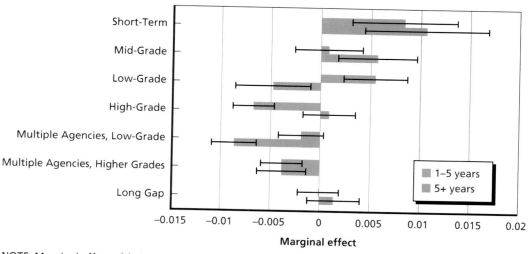

NOTE: Marginal effect of federal service at entry on probability of being in each career pattern. Results are based on a multinomial logistic regression of the probability of being in each career pattern, and can be interpreted as the percentage point difference in probability of career pattern membership, relative to individuals who initially entered with no prior federal service. Black bars indicate 95 percent confidence intervals. Authors' calculations based on hierarchical clustering and regression analysis using end-of-year snapshots from the DMDC Civilian Master Files from FY 1980 to FY 2015.
RAND *RR2280A-D.7c*

Entry Location

Figure D.8a shows the continuation rates for those who were first observed in the civilian workforce in the D.C. metropolitan area, versus those who were first observed elsewhere.[8] During the first five YOS, there is little difference in continuation probabilities between these groups. However, after five YOS, those who first entered in D.C. have slightly lower probabilities of continuation than those initially observed elsewhere. Figures D.8b and D.8c suggest that those who entered in D.C. are also more likely to be in the Short-Term career pattern and to be in higher grade levels.

Figure D.8a
Continuation Curves by Entry Location

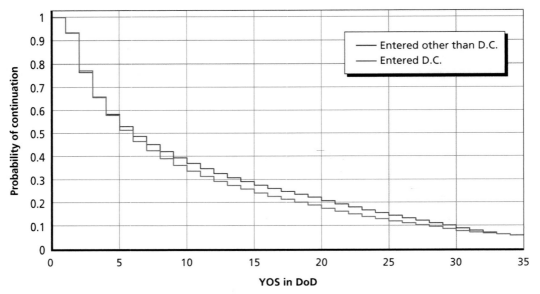

NOTE: Kaplan-Meier estimates, by entry location, of the continuation probabilities after each year of service for employees in the hierarchical cluster analysis. Individuals are identified as departing the first time they are no longer observed in an end-of-FY snapshot, and are observed until the end of FY 2015 or until they leave the DoD civilian workforce. Authors' calculations based on end-of-year snapshots from the DMDC Civilian Master Files from FY 1980 to FY 2015.
RAND *RR2280A-D.8a*

---

[8]   A log-rank test finds that the curves are statistically different for those who entered in D.C. versus those who did not ($p < .0001$).

Figure D.8b
Distribution of Career Patterns by Entry Location

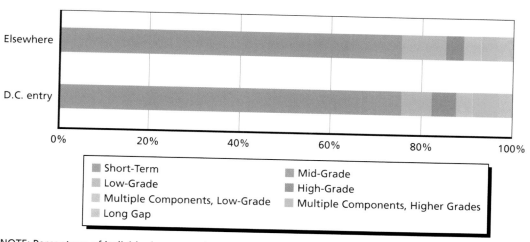

NOTE: Percentage of individual career trajectories identified with each career pattern, by entry location. Authors' calculations based on hierarchical clustering analysis using end-of-year snapshots from the DMDC Civilian Master Files from FY 1980 to FY 2015.
RAND RR2280A-D.8b

Figure D.8c
Marginal Effects of Entry in D.C. Metro Area (Relative to Entry in Another Location)

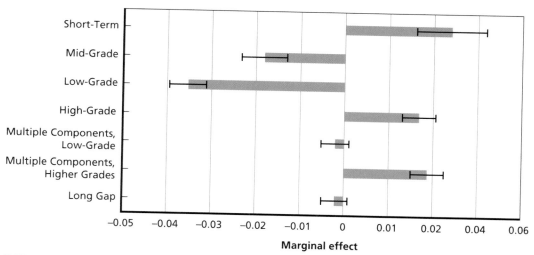

NOTE: Marginal effect of entry in the D.C. metro area on probability of being in each career pattern. Results are based on a multinomial logistic regression of the probability of being in each career pattern, and can be interpreted as the percentage point difference in probability of career pattern membership, relative to individuals who did not enter in the civilian workforce in D.C. Black bars indicate 95 percent confidence intervals. Authors' calculations based on hierarchical clustering and regression analysis using end-of-year snapshots from the DMDC Civilian Master Files from FY 1980 to FY 2015.
RAND RR2280A-D.8c

References

Abbott, Andrew, and Angela Tsay, "Sequence Analysis and Optimal Matching Methods in Sociology Review and Prospect," *Sociological Methods & Research*, Vol. 29, No. 1, 2000, pp. 3–33.

Asch, Beth J., Trey Miller, and Gariel Weinberger, *Can We Explain Gender Differences in Officer Career Progression?* Santa Monica, Calif.: RAND Corporation, RR-1288-OSD, 2016.

Blinder, Alan, "Wage Discrimination: Reduced Form and Structural Estimates," *Journal of Human Resources*, Vol. 8, 1973, pp. 436–455.

Bureau of Labor Statistics, "Employee Tenure Summary," September 22, 2016. As of September 23, 2016:
http://www.bls.gov/news.release/tenure.nr0.htm

Fortin, Nicole, Thomas Lemieux, and Sergio Firpo, "Decomposition Methods in Economics," in Orley Ashenfelter and David Card, eds., *Handbook of Labor Economics, Volume 4a*, Amsterdam: Elsevier B.V., 2011, pp. 1–102.

Maechler, Martin, Peter Rousseeuw, Anja Struyf, Mia Hubert, and Kurt Hornik, Cluster: Cluster Analysis Basics and Extension, R package version 2.0.3, 2015.

Murtagh, Fionn, and Pierre Legendre, "Ward's Hierarchical Agglomerative Clustering Method: Which Algorithms Implement Ward's Criterion," *Journal of Classification*, Vol. 31, No. 3, 2014, pp. 274–295.

Nataraj, Shanthi, Lawrence M. Hanser, Frank A. Camm, and Jessica M. Yeats, *The Future of the Army's Civilian Workforce: Comparing Projected Inventory with Anticipated Requirements and Estimating Cost Under Different Personnel Policies*, Santa Monica, Calif.: RAND Corporation, RR-576-A, 2014.

Oaxaca, Ronald, "Male-Female Wage Differentials in the Urban Labor Market," *International Economic Review*, Vol. 14, 1973, pp. 693–709.

Office of Personnel Management, *Handbook of Occupational Groups and Families*, Washington, D.C.: Office of Personnel Management, May 2009.

OPM—*See* Office of Personnel Management.

R Core Team, "R: A Language and Environment for Statistical Computing," R Foundation for Statistical Computing, Vienna, Austria, 2015. As of January 26, 2018:
https://www.R-project.org/

Ritschard, Gilbert, Reto Burgin, and Matthias Studer, "Exploratory Mining of Life Event Histories," in J. J. McArdle and G. Ritschard, eds., *Contemporary Issues in Exploratory Data Mining in the Behavioral Sciences*, New York: Routledge, 2013, pp. 221–253.

U.S. Army, Civilian Personnel Online, "National Security Personnel System," October 16, 2013. As of November 4, 2015:
http://cpol.army.mil/library/general/nsps/

U.S. Department of the Army, Career Program Management: Army Regulation 690-950, 2016.

Ward, Joe H., Jr., "Hierarchical Grouping to Optimize an Objective Function," *Journal of the American Statistical Association*, Vol. 58, 1963, pp. 236–244.